MICHAEL PHELPS

THE WORLD'S GREATEST OLYMPIAN

TRIUMPH
BOOKS

USA
TODAY
usatoday.com

Phelps drowns the competition

Swimmer stays on track with world record in 200 free, part of seven-medal day for USA

By Vicki Michaelis • Date: August 12, 2008

BEIJING — This time, Michael Phelps made it look easy.

Phelps continued his run toward a record eight Olympic gold medals with a never-in-doubt victory in the 200-meter freestyle, the only individual event he didn't win in the 2004 Olympics.

Phelps was ahead by nearly half a second at the first turn and ended up lowering his world record, winning in 1 minute, 42.96 seconds. Silver medalist Park Tae Hwan of South Korea was nearly two seconds back, at 1:44.85, and the USA's Peter Vanderkaay was third in 1:45.14.

Phelps' victory led a dominating day for U.S. swimmers at the Water Cube. The USA won seven medals, three of them gold.

"What Michael's doing, it's elevating everybody else's performance here," said Aaron Peirsol, who also lowered his world record, to 52.54 seconds, while defending his Olympic gold in the 100 backstroke. American Matt Grevers won silver.

In the women's 100 backstroke, Natalie Coughlin won her second consecutive Olympic gold in a U.S. record 58.96 seconds, with teammate Margaret Hoelzer winning bronze. Rebecca Soni added a silver in the 100 breaststroke.

Phelps' victory gave him his third gold of the Beijing

Phelps' drive for eight golds gained steam in his third race as he scorched the water in the 200-meter freestyle with a world record time of 1:42:96.

Olympics, keeping him on track to surpass Mark Spitz's seven golds from the 1972 Olympics.

It also gave Phelps his ninth career Olympic gold, tying him for the all-time record with Spitz, U.S. track and field star Carl Lewis, Finnish runner Paavo Nurmi and Ukrainian gymnast Larysa Latynina.

"It's a pretty amazing accomplishment," said Phelps, who could stand alone in the career gold count after his two events Wednesday, the 200-meter butterfly and 4x200-meter freestyle relay.

The comfortable victory for Phelps was in sharp contrast to the 200 freestyle he contested in 2004. At that Games, he finished third behind Australian superstar Ian Thorpe and Pieter van den Hoogenband, the 2000 Olympic champion.

At last year's worlds, he broke Thorpe's world record in the event while finishing more than two seconds ahead of van den Hoogenband.

Thorpe's November 2006 retirement and van den Hoogenband's decision to drop the 200 freestyle from his Beijing Olympic program left a somewhat depleted field to challenge Phelps. That didn't diminish the effect of his yawning gap of victory.

"He's not just winning but destroying everything," Peirsol said. "It's awesome to watch."

Records fall

Just four days into the swimming competition, 10 world records have been set in the Water Cube pool, two more than the entire 2004 Olympic meet.

Phelps and Peirsol each broke his own record in the 200 freestyle and 100 backstroke, respectively. Peirsol shaved 35/100th of a second off the record he set in the Olympic trials in June.

U.S. swimmers have set five of the world records, including two by Phelps (also in the 400 individual medley) and two by the U.S. 4x100 freestyle relay.

"This meet is unbelievable," U.S. Olympic women's coach Jack Bauerle said. "This has changed the lay of the land in what we think is fast."

Jason Lezak's superhuman anchor leg in the men's 4x100 freestyle relay final Monday kept Phelps' quest for eight Olympic golds on track. But Lezak was more motivated to re-establish U.S. relay dominance than to assist Phelps in his march toward the record books.

"I've been a part of the two teams at the last two Olympics that came out behind," the 32-year-old said, "and I think I wanted it more than anybody — not just for myself but to show that we are the nation to beat in that relay." ✎

With the field behind him in every race he swam, Phelps couldn't help but look over his shoulder during his march toward history in the Beijing Olympics.

Phelps always a team player

Superstar prefers sharing spotlight with teammates

By Christine Brennan • Date: August 12, 2008

BEIJING — Michael Phelps is a team guy trapped in an individual sport. If all eight of his Olympic swims could be relays, he would be a very happy young man.

"The relays are the funnest events," he says. In the language of an uncomplicated 23-year-old — Phelps-speak, if you will — that tells you just about all you need to know about the nation's most famous Olympian.

How fitting, then, that it was the team around him that kept Phelps' quest for eight Olympic gold medals afloat for another day before he went out and won another individual race, the 200-meter freestyle, in world-record time.

Phelps was a mere spectator on the pool deck when gold medal No. 2 was won for him and his country by Jason Lezak, a relay veteran and a bit of a journeyman who gritted his teeth and reeled in French world recordholder Alain Bernard after being behind by half a body length with less than 25 seconds of swimming remaining.

The primal scream that Phelps let out when Lezak touched the wall first was real, but he wasn't celebrating keeping his gold medal quest alive. Phelps doesn't think like that, at least not initially. No, he was delirious because he was sharing a monumental victory with three of his pals, simple as that.

The United States wins the gold medal in the 4x100 medley relay at the National Aquatics Center. Left to right are Phelps, Brendan Hansen, Aaron Peirsol and Jason Lezak. Phelps earned his eighth gold medal of the Beijing Olympic Games, breaking swimmer Mark Spitz's seven Olympic gold medal mark from 1972.

"Going up there with four guys, we were really one," Phelps said after having had eight hours to digest what the relay team had accomplished. "We all had to swim the perfect race, and we swam that perfect race today."

He had already seen replays of his reaction as Lezak touched out Bernard by eight-hundredths of a second. "I let out a pretty fierce yell. It just shows how emotional that race was and how excited we were. It was just an amazing race. ... We had to do everything as a team to win that race, and we did."

We. There was that word, over and over again. In Phelps' line of work, it's a word often left unsaid, but it's a word he'd love to overuse. His coach, Bob Bowman, noticed that immediately — just how happy the individualist was when playing with the group.

"I think he likes the aspect of having it not be about him, because so much of it is," Bowman said. "I think he loves that. He loves getting with those guys. And he likes team sports. He likes watching basketball and football. This is the one time he gets to really be a part of something."

Phelps played some team sports as a boy, "but nothing really major." There was a reason why, he said in a November interview with USA TODAY's Vicki Michaelis:

"I would say outside the pool, I'm not really that flexible. I don't know what it is. There are things I can't do out of the water that other people can do. It's completely different in the water. You put me in another sport, I can get by, but it's not the best situation.

"In basketball, I had the height, that's about it. I can't dunk, and I'm 6' 4". That's pretty pathetic. Baseball, I don't know if it's like moving different ways to get to the ball, sliding, whatever, but it's not me. ... I don't have very much hand-eye coordination either."

It's rather nice to know a geek can hit it big at the Olympics, isn't it?

That's the subtle charm of Phelps, who seems perfectly suited to the life he is leading: sleep, eat, swim, sleep some more, eat some more, play Spades, watch movies, do it all over again. He is truly liked by his teammates, which certainly can be a motivating factor when they are churning through the water, fighting like crazy for him and the rest of the team.

Within minutes of winning the relay gold, the four teammates were already teasing Phelps about what he would owe Lezak if Phelps does indeed go on to win the eight golds and earn Speedo's promised $1 million bonus. At least an eighth?

Lezak dismissed the thought. "We were a team out there," Lezak said. "Michael can keep whatever he gets. ... I think Michael knows we didn't do this for him, but he's a part of it, whether he wins eight gold medals or not."

Phelps and teammates wave to the crowd while being announced during the awards ceremony for the 4x100-meter medley relay final.

On top, past all the greats

As fog clears, Phelps sees the majesty of his achievement

By Vicki Michaelis; Mike Dodd • Date: August 14, 2008

BEIJING — Michael Phelps couldn't see at the moment he became the Olympian with the most gold medals, but he is starting to get a clearer vision of his place in Olympic history.

Phelps' goggles began filling with water when he dove in for the 200-meter butterfly final. He couldn't see as he approached the last turn and finish.

"I was just hoping that I was winning," he said.

Indeed he was, and in world-record time. Within an hour, after a goggle adjustment, he was back in the pool, leading off a 4x200 freestyle relay team that won by more than 5 seconds and set another world record, posting the first sub-7-minute finish ever.

Phelps now has five golds in his Beijing Olympic collection, more than halfway to surpassing Mark Spitz's record seven golds from the 1972 Munich Olympics.

The victories gave Phelps career Olympic golds Nos. 10 and 11, vaulting him past Spitz, U.S. track star Carl Lewis, Finnish runner Paavo Nurmi and Ukrainian gymnast Larysa Latynina for the all-time record.

"When I was at the awards ceremony for the 200 fly, I started thinking about it, and that's when I started tearing up," Phelps said. "To be at the top with so many great athletes who

Phelps lowers his head during the playing of the national anthem after winning the gold medal in the 200-meter individual medley final in Beijing.

have walked in these Olympic Games, it's a pretty amazing feeling."

Phelps also is the most decorated U.S. Olympian, with 13 medals overall. He won six gold and two bronze medals in 2004 at Athens. Swimmer Jenny Thompson was the previous recordholder, with 12 Olympic medals.

As Spitz did in 1972, Phelps has set world records in every event he's swum in Beijing.

He won the 200 butterfly Wednesday in 1 minute, 52.03 seconds to lower his own world record and hold off silver medalist Laszlo Cseh of Hungary, who finished in 1:52.70. ✎

1:52.03

Phelps' world record time in the 200-meter butterfly.

(opposite) Phelps cheers on a teammate during a relay heat in Beijing. (above) Even President Bush became a swimming fan during Phelps' remarkable performance in Beijing.

Phelps' sixth leads gold rush

Sets world mark in 200 IM

By Vicki Michaelis • Date: August 15, 2008

BEIJING — With 200 more meters of otherworldly swimming, Michael Phelps could clinch the greatest Olympic performance ever.

After a win in the 200-meter individual medley, Phelps has six gold medals in the Beijing Olympics and two more races in his quest for eight golds.

In his quest to make history in the pool, Phelps competes Saturday morning in the 100 butterfly final. If he finishes ahead of teammate Ian Crocker in that race, he is expected to swim Sunday with the U.S. men in the 4x100 medley relay final.

With victories in both, Phelps would top the record seven gold medals won by Mark Spitz in the 1972 Olympics.

Like Spitz, Phelps has set a world record in every final he's raced in Beijing. He lowered his world record in the 200 IM to 1minute, 54.23 seconds to finish ahead of silver medalist Laszlo Cseh of Hungary and U.S. teammate Ryan Lochte, who won bronze.

"It's never a relief," Phelps said after the 200 IM win. "Tomorrow is going to be a very tough race."

Cseh has finished second to Phelps in three races in Beijing. "Maybe next time, I can catch him," Cseh said.

Lochte finished behind Phelps in the 200 IM, but he did

Phelps waves a U.S. flag as he walks around the pool deck after the medal ceremony with his teammates. The United States won the gold medal in the 4x100 medley relay at the National Aquatics Center in Beijing, China. Aaron Peirsol, Brendan Hansen, Michael Phelps and Jason Lezak swam in the final. Phelps earned his eighth gold medal of the Beijing Olympic Games, breaking swimmer Mark Spitz's seven Olympic gold medal mark from 1972.

win his first individual Olympic gold medal earlier in the morning, beating U.S. teammate Aaron Peirsol in the 200 backstroke.

Lochte won in a world-record 1:53.94. Peirsol, the 2004 Olympic champion, finished in 1:54.33.

Rebecca Soni's surprise victory today in the 200 breaststroke, edging Australian favorite Leisel Jones in a world-record 2:20.22, lifted the spirits of the U.S. women's team after medal contenders Katie Hoff and Kate Ziegler failed to qualify for the 800 freestyle final.

If all that glitters around Phelps' neck in Beijing is gold, Spitz will have to cede his spot in the record books.

"I'm saying to myself, 'Hey, it's OK, records are made to be broken, including mine,'" Spitz said this summer. "Thirty-six years is a long time." ∾

To Phelps, Lil' Wayne is music of champions

Something in the words and music of an R-rated rapper from New Orleans apparently speaks to the American demigod from Baltimore.

If the end of every race finds Michael Phelps gazing up at the scoreboard, thrusting a finger skyward celebrating another world record, the lasting prerace image is him walking onto the Water Cube deck drawing last-minute inspiration from ... Lil' Wayne on his iPod.

Phelps identified him as his artist of choice after qualifying for the 200-meter individual medley final, the sixth of his eight events in Beijing. Earlier, on *The Today Show* on NBC, he expressed specific fondness for Lil' Wayne's "I'm Me," off the rapper's five-track album *The Leak*.

From some of the (less explicit) lyrics, the connection is clear:

"Yes, I'm the best, and I ain't

positive, I'm definite

I know the game like I'm reffing it

This is Tha Carter, Tha Carter 3, the new testament

And I'm the God, and this is what I bless them with ...

I'm me, I'm me, I'm me, I'm me

Baby, I'm me, so why you? You're not me, you're not me

And I know that ain't fair, but I don't care

I'm a ... Cash Money millionaire."

Says Lil' Wayne of Phelps: "I was like, 'For real?' Mike Phelps is listening to Weezy ... That's what's up ... Mike is doing his thing, and I'm doing my thing."

Phelps hugs his mom as they celebrate winning another gold medal at the Beijing Olympics.

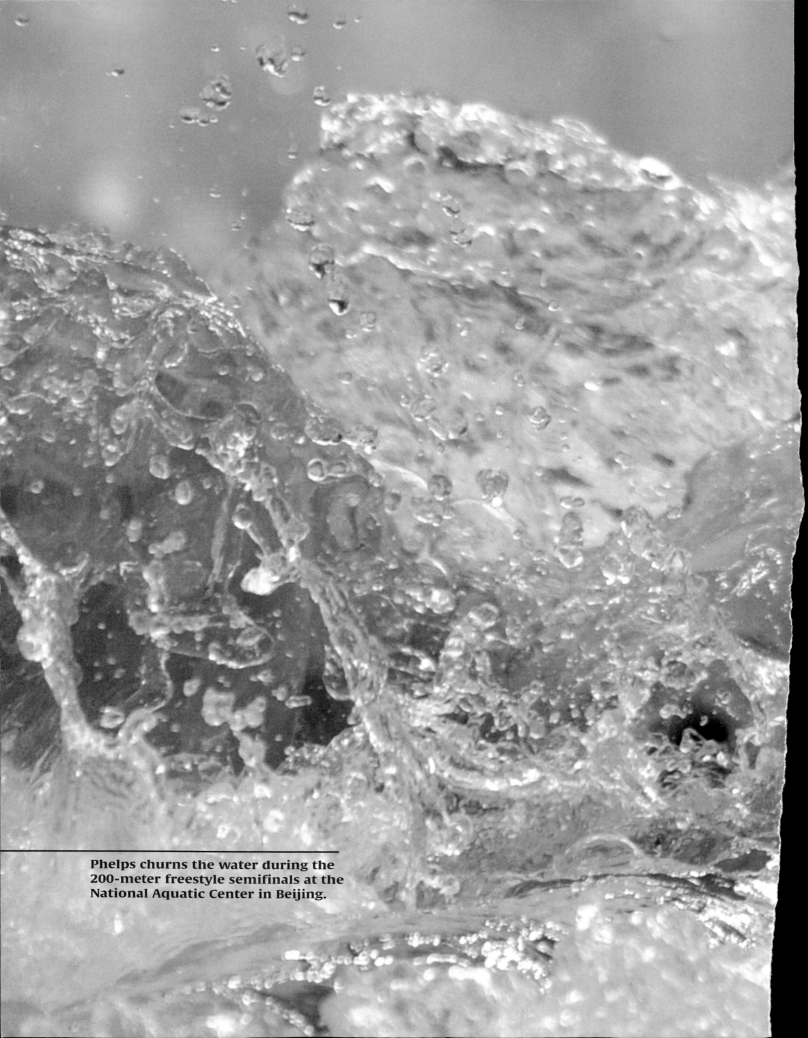

Phelps churns the water during the 200-meter freestyle semifinals at the National Aquatic Center in Beijing.

Phelps' 2008 Beijing Olympics swim results

08/09	Men's 400m Medley Qualification - Heat 4		4:07.82 (1st)
08/10	Men's 400m Medley Final		Gold 4:03.84 (1st)
08/10	Men's 200m Freestyle - Heat 8		1:46.48 (2nd)
08/10	Men's 200m Freestyle Semifinal 2		1:46.28 (3rd)
08/11	Men's 4 x 100m Free Final		Gold 3:08.24 (1st)
08/11	Men's 200m Butterfly - Heat 6		1:53.70 (1st)
08/12	Men's 200m Free Final		Gold 1:42.96 (1st)
08/11	Men's 200m Butterfly Semifinal - Heat 2		1:53.70 (1st)
08/13	Men's 200m Butterfly Final		Gold 1:52.03 (1st)
08/13	Men's 4 x 200m Free Final		Gold 6:58.56 (1st)
08/14	Men's 200m Medley Qualification - Heat 6		1:58.65 (1st)
08/14	Men's 200m Medley Semifinal - Heat 1		1:57.70 (1st)
08/14	Men's 100m Butterfly Qualification - Heat 9		50.87 (2nd)
08/15	Men's 200m Medley Final		Gold 1:54.23 (1st)
08/15	Men's 100m Butterfly Semifinal - Heat 1		50.97 (1st)
08/15	Men's 100m Butterfly Final		Gold 50.58 (1st)
08/17	Men's 4 x 100m Medley Final		Gold 3:29.34 (1st)

This book is available in quantity at special discounts for your group
or organization. For further information, contact:

Triumph Books
542 South Dearborn Street
Suite 750
Chicago, Illinois 60605
(312) 939-3330
Fax (312) 663-3557

Printed in United States of America
ISBN: 978-1-60078-225-1

Photos courtesy of USA TODAY unless otherwise indicated

Content packaged by Mojo Media, Inc.
Joe Funk: Editor
Jason Hinman: Creative Director

Contents

About this book:
This book features a collection of stories about Michael Phelps, from the splashy debut he made as a gangly Baltimore teenager in the early 2000s, to his eight gold medals in Beijing and ascendance as arguably one of the greatest Olympic athletes in history, as told by the award-winning writers, editors and photographers of USA TODAY.

(left) Phelps and the rest of the field start the 400-meter individual medley on the first day of swimming competition in Beijing.

(previous spread) This combination of photos shows Michael Phelps holding each of his eight gold medals after (top, left to right) the 400-meter individual medley, 4x100-meter freestyle relay, 200-meter freestyle, 200-meter butterfly, (bottom, left to right) 4x200-meter freestyle relay, 200-meter individual medley, 100m butterfly and the 4x100-meter medley relay at the 2008 Olympics in Beijing.

A Phelps surfaces on rare occasion

Olympic feats few and far between

By Christine Brennan • Date: August 18, 2008

BEIJING — One of the reasons we fall in love with Olympic athletes is that they never overstay their welcome. They drop into our lives for two weeks every four years, then they drop right out again. They don't play a 162-game schedule. Their season doesn't stretch from September until early February. They don't go on strike. They rarely complain about their contracts (if they even have contracts).

Basically, they show up, compete for a few days, then leave. Often, we never see them again, and, for the most part, that's just fine with us.

So what, then, do we make of the future of Michael Phelps? He has been such a part of the lives of so many Americans for the past week that we almost can't let him go. Yet we must, because the Water Cube has gone dark, at least for swimming, and Phelps will leave Beijing on Thursday to head to London, then home to Leno, then ... what, exactly?

Some lucrative corporate appearances, certainly. Commercials? Absolutely. A parade through Baltimore? Guaranteed.

But because Phelps swims, the vast majority of the people who planned their nightly schedules around his races for the past week will not see him compete for another four years, until the 2012 London Olympics, which Phelps says he plans to attend.

In eight shining moments at the Beijing Olympics, Phelps made us all proud to be Americans.

There is no pro swimming league, no Baltimore Backstrokers against the Fort Lauderdale Freestylers. And no one is clamoring for someone to start such an enterprise. College and pro football are just around the corner, while baseball enters the final weeks of its playoff races.

Swimming? It will fall off the radar screen almost as quickly as it appeared a little more than a week ago. There are next year's national championships, and the worlds, but those events often aren't televised, even with Phelps in them — and he plans to be at both next year. And if they are televised, the ratings will be paltry, simply because it's not the Olympics.

These truths, however, do not diminish anything Phelps accomplished over the nine magical days of Olympic swimming. If anything, they enhance what he did.

Most professional athletes get a chance to reach their sport's greatest heights once every 52 weeks. Olympians like Phelps are on the 208-week plan. What they achieve becomes more memorable because they waited so long to do it.

"I wanted to make sure I took every single moment in," Phelps said, and he meant it, from the card games with his Olympic Village roommates to all eight visits to the medal stand. "I don't want to forget anything that happened."

If he did this every year, he'd never think like that.

Phelps already is a multimillionaire, and there are no limits for him as an all-American pitchman, if he wants to do that. But there's a little bit of Eric Heiden in Michael Phelps. You remember Heiden? He won five speed skating gold medals at the 1980 Lake Placid Olympics, then eschewed all endorsements to go to medical school.

Phelps isn't doing that. He certainly isn't saying no to everyone — not even close — but when asked what he looked forward to now that his races were over, he didn't speak of Disney World or TV shows or photo shoots. No, he talked about literally sitting down and "not moving," about spending time with his mother, his two sisters and his good friends.

High-maintenance, this man is not.

Yet for as much as he is looking forward to putting up his feet, he'll miss this. And we will miss him. So let's put his performances on a shelf with the greatest things we will ever remember about sports, and let's make sure they remain there, a lovely memory, to be cherished forever.

And one other thing: His pledge to compete in London in 2012?

Let's hold him to that one. ❧

Phelps celebrates with Garrett Weber-Gale, right, as the USA comes from behind—thanks to USA anchor swimmer Jason Lezak, in water—to win the gold in the men's 4x100-meter freestyle relay finals at the National Aquatic Center in Beijing.

London calling: Phelps set sights on 2012

Mission accomplished, encore could include new events

By Vicki Michaelis • Date: August 18, 2008

BEIJING — Four years from now, as the 2012 Summer Olympics are about to begin, the buzz could be about Michael Phelps trying to match an eminent Olympic record.

His own.

In the Beijing Olympics, Phelps won eight gold medals, setting the single-Games gold standard so high it seems unlikely anyone could reach it or surpass it anytime soon — anyone but Phelps himself, that is.

Phelps has planned all along to continue competing through the 2012 Olympics, when he will be 27. Whether he would compete in eight events again remains to be seen.

"It might be ambitious," Bob Bowman, Phelps' coach, says of his possible 2012 program, "but just different events maybe. And I don't know if it could be this ambitious."

With three more medals in London, Phelps would achieve the only Olympic medals record that he doesn't own. Including his six gold and two bronze medals from 2004, Phelps has 16 Olympic medals, two shy of the record 18 won by Soviet gymnast Larysa Latynina.

"I'd like to try some new events and just see what happens with them," Phelps said. "Bob has said that he wants to start fresh, do things that he hasn't done before — try new things in workout, try new training methods."

Phelps wins the gold medal in the men's 100-meter butterfly, giving him seven gold medals and matching Mark Spitz's Olympic record.

Phelps says he would like to drop the 400-meter individual medley from his program and swim all shorter-distance races. He could end up dropping other events from his program — perhaps some he consistently wins by wide margins, such as the 200 freestyle and 200 butterfly — and adding events that would present more of a challenge.

"For him to continue to do this and enjoy it, which is now really very important to me and him, I think he needs to switch it up some. We'll have to see, maybe experiment," Bowman says.

Before the Beijing Olympics, Phelps and Bowman said this Games would be his prime time to rewrite the record books. Neither is certain Phelps in four years would be as capable or as willing to devote himself to the kind of training he did before Beijing. In peak weeks, he swam 80,000 meters (49.7 miles).

It's no wonder Phelps' short-term plan was not ambitious at all.

"I'm going to take a vacation where I won't do anything," says Phelps, who plans to leave Beijing on Thursday, which means he won't participate in the closing ceremony. "I'll sit around, and I won't have to go anywhere, be anywhere at a special time."

In no time, though, he's sure to be back in the pool. He and Bowman are moving from Ann Arbor, Mich., where Bowman was head coach of the University of Michigan men's swimming team, back to Phelps' roots in Baltimore.

Bowman has a new job as chief executive at the North Baltimore Aquatic Club, allowing him and Phelps to return to the swim club where they first began working together when Phelps was 11. Bowman will continue coaching Phelps.

The move also will put Phelps nearer to Debbie Phelps, a principal at a middle school in Baltimore who raised him and his two sisters as a single mother. She was a constant presence at the Water Cube as he swam toward history, although they had no chance to celebrate together until he was done.

After he swam his last race in Beijing, Phelps said, "I kind of just want to see my mom."

He plans to return to swimming in time to qualify for next year's world championships, which will begin in mid-July in Rome.

"My mom's told me that I better make the team because she wants to go to Rome," Phelps says.

That worlds meet should offer the first glimpse of what Phelps and Bowman might be experimenting with as they look toward the London Games.

Jon Urbanchek, Bowman's predecessor at Michigan who helped coach Phelps in

By focusing on shorter sprint races, Phelps just might dominate again in 2012.

recent years, says he expects Phelps won't swim any races longer than 200 meters in 2012 and "perhaps just the 100 free, 100 back and 100 fly."

The 100 butterfly was the only one of the three on Phelps' Beijing program. It was the only event in which he didn't break the world record. In fact, he needed a miraculous finish to win by one one-hundredth of a second over silver medalist Milorad Cavic of Serbia.

Phelps didn't compete in the 100 freestyle in Beijing, but he did swim the leadoff leg in the 4x100 freestyle relay. His time of 47.51 seconds would have been fast enough for a bronze medal in the Beijing men's 100 freestyle final.

Phelps also swam the eighth-fastest time (53.01) in the 100 backstroke this year. That is less than a half a second off the world record Aaron Peirsol set (52.54) while winning gold in Beijing.

Phelps' swim in the 100 butterfly final showed why 100-meter races could be just the challenge he needs to keep him motivated through four more years of early wake-up calls and hard workouts.

Phelps doesn't have sprinter's speed. That's partly because his training has been geared more toward endurance, to prepare him for the 17 swims he had to complete over the nine days of the Beijing Olympics.

At the turn of the 100 butterfly final, he was in seventh place.

He drew on his endurance fitness to close, and then he finished first only by taking a fast, half-stroke at the end, which carried him into the touch pad with more force than the gliding Cavic.

If Phelps is to become a sprinter, which is the natural course for swimmers as they get older because the training tends to be less taxing, he will have to become better at the start and faster in the first 50 meters. In shorter races, with fewer turns, he won't be able to get as much of an edge as he does now on his underwater distance off the walls.

"He thinks it might be a little easier," Bowman says of sprint training, "but it will be different. I think he can sprint, but I think he's more naturally suited to longer events, so it'll be a change for him, but I think a good one."

Good enough for another eight golds?

Check back four years from now. ﹏

In one of the most memorable moments of the Beijing Olympics, Phelps, left, just barely out-touches Milorad Cavic of Serbia in the 100-meter butterfly final.

Can Phelps ever be topped?

In Beijing, the stars aligned for a unique talent to make Olympic history. Here's why it's unlikely to happen again anytime soon.

By Vicki Michaelis • Date: August 15, 2008

BEIJING — NBA star Kobe Bryant was at the National Aquatics Center this week when Michael Phelps won his fourth and fifth gold medals of the Beijing Olympics.

Bryant turned to several swimmers sitting near him for guidance on what he was watching.

"It's the first time I've ever been at a swimming event, and I said, 'This can't be normal,'" he says. "And they said, 'It's not normal. This is history in the making.'"

Whether or not Phelps wins eight gold medals in Beijing to surpass Mark Spitz's record seven golds from the 1972 Games, his audacious march toward Olympic history and his astounding performances are unlikely to be matched for years — if ever. As Spitz did 36 years ago in Munich — when the depth of swimming talent wasn't nearly what it is now — Phelps is setting a world record in every event he swims.

His success represents one of those rare moments in sports when the stars align to produce an awe-inspiring feat: an athlete with unique talent, focus, stamina and versatility, fast in each of swimming's four strokes at a time when specialization and growth of the sport worldwide have made it tougher than ever to be dominant.

"If I see it again, I'll be shocked," fellow U.S. Olympic swimmer Erik Vendt says of Phelps' gold rush.

Phelps rushes through the water in the men's 4x100-meter medley relay final at the National Aquatics Center in Beijing.

Carmelo Anthony, Bryant's teammate on the U.S. basketball team, compares Phelps' results to Michael Jordan winning six NBA titles. "He's amazing," Anthony says.

Heading into the weekend, Phelps, 23, had broken the Olympic record for total gold medals (12, having won six in the 2004 Games and six this week). He had two events left in Beijing, the 100 butterfly and the 4x100 medley relay.

His 14 total Olympic medals are third on the all-time list, behind the 18 by Soviet gymnast Larysa Latynina from 1956 to 1964 and the 15 by another Soviet gymnast, Nikolai Andrianov, from 1972 to 1980. In Beijing, Phelps has passed several Olympians on the all-time winners' list, including U.S. swimmer Jenny Thompson, who won 12 medals from 1992 to 2004.

For all his ability, Phelps' success at collecting medals also reflects how there are more chances to win medals in swimming than virtually any other sport, and how factors beyond Phelps' control have broken his way. Chief among them: the strength of the U.S. men's team, whose success in relays gives Phelps medal opportunities he would not have swimming for another country. That was never more clear than when Jason Lezak's dramatic finish Monday, edging Frenchman Alain Bernard in the 4x100 freestyle relay, kept Phelps' pursuit on track.

"I don't know that we'll ever see it in our lifetime," U.S. national swim team coach Mark Schubert says of Phelps' pursuit. "We have to cherish it as we watch it."

After winning the 200-meter individual medley today in Beijing, Phelps is two golds away from the record. Phelps' toughest remaining challenge could come when he will face U.S. teammate Ian Crocker in the 100 butterfly. Crocker is the only swimmer besides Phelps to hold the world record in an event Phelps swims. Phelps edged Crocker in the 100 butterfly in the 2004 Games and last year's world championships.

Phelps' Olympics wrap up with the 4x100 medley relay. The U.S. men have never lost the medley relay in the Olympics and are heavily favored.

"I take it one race at a time," Phelps says. "That's the only thing I can do right now."

Following that mantra became somewhat difficult even for the uber-focused Phelps as, victory by victory, he reached historical markers this week. After his win in the 200 butterfly gave him more career gold medals than any other Olympian, he had less than an hour to prepare for swimming the leadoff leg in the 4x200 freestyle relay.

"I was trying to focus on my next race, but I kept thinking, 'Wow, greatest Olympian of all time.' It's a pretty cool title."

If Phelps adds eight gold medals to his collection in Beijing, he will have a total of 14 golds. Second on the list, all tied at nine, are

Phelps shouts encouragement to Peter Vanderkaay on the last leg of their gold medal win in the men's 4x200 freestyle relay final at the National Aquatics Center in Beijing. The USA smashed the old world record by 4.68 seconds.

Spitz (who competed in the 1968 and 1972 Games), Latynina, Finnish runner Paavo Nurmi (1920–28) and U.S. track and field star Carl Lewis (1984–96).

'Truly a special individual'

Swimmers, gymnasts and track and field athletes dominate the Olympic medal records because they can compete in multiple individual events and boost their medal totals with team events, such as relays. Phelps has five individual events and three relays on his Beijing program.

Swimming the same program in the 2004 Olympics, Phelps won six gold and two bronze medals. The eight medals were the most won by an athlete in a single, non-boycotted Games.

The records Phelps is setting in Beijing could stand for a long time. USA Swimming has other multiple-event swimmers, such as Ryan Lochte and Katie Hoff, medaling at the Olympic level. But Schubert doesn't see anyone in the pipeline who could take on what Phelps has.

"I think you have to be realistic as to how incredible this effort is," Schubert says. "It has to do with his physical ability, his ability to race, his ability to keep his focus, to get excited when he needs to get excited, to get down when he needs to get down."

Phelps, with an extraordinarily long torso, extreme flexibility and a 6' 7" wingspan, grew up with two older sisters who were top-level swimmers. He began training as a kid at the North Baltimore Aquatic Club, known for developing multi-event swimmers. Many clubs tend to point swimmers toward one swim stroke so they become competitive more quickly and can focus their energy on a specialty.

Phelps can beat the world's best butterflyers, freestylers and backstrokers, and in winning the 400 individual medley in Beijing, he showed top form in the breaststroke as well.

By age 11, Phelps was under the tutelage of Bob Bowman, a coach who saw his potential and began preparing him to stay steady under pressure.

"This is truly a special individual," U.S. Olympic Committee chief of sport performance Steve Roush says of Phelps, "with talent that is tough to comprehend."

In gymnastics and track and field, winning eight medals of any color at a single Olympics would be nearly impossible.

Among gymnasts, only the men would have a chance, because women compete in just four individual events. A male gymnast would have to medal in every one of the six individual events (rings, pommel horse, vault, parallel bars, floor exercise and high bar) as well as in the all-around and team competitions.

In track and field, an athlete would have to compete in running events and field events such as jumps, as Lewis did.

Both sports can take more of a toll on

athletes' bodies than swimming, making it tough for gymnasts and track and field stars to compete in as many events as Phelps, even if they could. Defending Olympic all-around gymnastics champion Paul Hamm of the USA had to withdraw from the Beijing Olympics because of injuries.

"To maintain a high level of performance over two or three Olympic Games is very, very difficult," U.S. men's gymnastics coach Kevin Mazeika says.

Phelps plans to compete at the 2012 London Olympics, which would be his fourth Games. At 15, he swam the 200 butterfly in 2000, finishing fifth.

He is unlikely to repeat his Beijing program in London; he's said he'll probably drop the grueling 400 individual medley. But he could replace it with a shorter event, such as the 100 freestyle or one of the backstroke events (the 100 or 200), and compete for eight medals again.

"Anything's possible, the way that he works," Bowman says.

Going into London, the only Olympic medal record Phelps might have yet to reach is Latynina's mark for career Olympic medals of any color. "If Michael sticks around for 2012 ... it's going to set the bar incredibly high," Roush says.

Olympic historian Bill Mallon calls medal records by swimmers and gymnasts "a little artificial" because they can be in so many events. But the possibility another swimmer will challenge Phelps' records any time soon seems remote.

In Australia, where swimming's popularity rivals football's in the USA, they're marveling at the one they call "Phelpsie."

"I don't want to say he does it effortlessly, but he does it beautifully," says Alan Thompson, head coach of Australia's swim team. "I'm not sure I'll see another one as good as he in my lifetime."

Competition is gaining

Swimming coaches are seeing medal contenders come from all corners of the world as various nations, recognizing the multiple-medal potential of the sport, invest more in swimming.

As the world gets better, "the impetus to specialize is definitely going to be there," Bowman says, "because if you spread yourself too thin, you're probably going to sacrifice your best event."

In Beijing, Park Tae-hwan became the first Olympic gold medalist in swimming from South Korea when he won the 400 freestyle. The French men, who nearly defeated the USA in the 4x100 freestyle relay, won their first relay medal in that event. Bernard, the anchor of the relay, went on to win the 100 freestyle.

Chinese athletes have won a few swimming medals in this Olympics as well, which could signal a new threat to Phelps' marks in the years ahead. Only a few countries, such as

Australia, and soon perhaps China, would be able to produce not only the athlete but a team good enough to get the necessary relay wins.

"Based on the way they're coming on," Roush says of China, "I would say there's a distinct possibility."

As for what Phelps is doing now, Spitz acknowledges Phelps faces many more obstacles than Spitz did when he won a record seven golds in the 1972 Games. In 100- and 200-meter events, swimmers now must compete in preliminaries and semifinals, rather than in just one qualifying heat, to reach the final.

Phelps will swim up to 17 times in Beijing. With warm-up and warm-down swims included, he will swim about 70,000 meters in Beijing. "For most people, that's a very hard training week," Schubert says.

In Spitz's era, the U.S. men were more dominant than they are now, making his three relay golds almost a given.

"He's showing a different kind of courage than I did," Spitz says. "I was not chasing Mark Spitz's record. I was chasing (swimmer) Don Schollander and Jesse Owens (who each won four golds at a single Olympics). When I came up with a program of seven, it seemed to be almost ridiculously invented by myself."

Phelps encountered an unforeseen obstacle in the 200 butterfly final Wednesday — his goggles filled with water, so he had to race without being able to see, counting strokes so he would know when to make turns at the wall. He still set a world record.

"It definitely never, ever gets old listening to the national anthem play," he says, "with a gold medal around your neck." ❧

(opposite) Phelps celebrates at the medals ceremony for the men's 400-meter individual medley at the National Aquatics Center in Beijing. (above) The spectacular National Aquatics Center, also known as The Water Cube, was a fitting venue for Phelps to break so many records.

Early years

Hard work in pool keeps teen phenom grounded

Phelps just normal high schooler with pro contract

By Vicki Michaelis • Date: August 13, 2003

Olympic sports

He has a year left of high school. He lives at home with his mom. Some of his friends work jobs at the mall. Some of his teammates are 13-year-old girls.

Not the typical life of a pro athlete.

But that's what 17-year-old swimmer Michael Phelps is after signing a contract with Speedo last fall. He even owns the pro athlete's ride of choice, a Cadillac Escalade, although it's used, a 2000 model. Mom insisted.

"A car is a car is a car to me," Debbie Phelps says.

In the last year, her son has grown to 6' 4", his feet to size 14, his bank account to heady figures and his sport status to phenom level. If his sport were basketball, scouts would be three-deep at his practices, and Akron (Ohio) St. Vincent-St. Mary basketball star LeBron James would be the second-best high school prospect in the USA.

Yet it's not often Debbie Phelps needs to serve up a side of ego-busting at the dinner table in Baltimore.

Logging thousands of solitary laps, day after day, meter after meter, can keep a guy grounded — even a teenage one with his name signed to an endorsement deal.

"I eat a lot, I sleep a lot, obviously I swim a lot," Phelps says.

At 15 years old during the Sydney Games, Phelps was the youngest male swimmer to make the U.S. Olympic team since 1932.

"I'm a normal 17-year-old kid." Mom says so, too: Her son still uses his fingers to clean every last bit of ice cream out of a sundae bowl.

Phelps is paranormal in the water, last year becoming the youngest male, at 15 years, nine months, to set a world swimming record. The mark came in the 200-meter butterfly. He lowered it at the 2001 world championships, to 1:54.58.

At the Phillips 66 U.S. National Swimming Championships in Fort Lauderdale, Phelps set a U.S. record in winning the 200- meter individual medley.

But by the 2004 Summer Olympics, the 200 fly is likely to be just one event among several in which Phelps is a favorite.

"Probably since Mark Spitz he's the first guy we have with multiple talents," says University of Michigan men's coach Jon Urbanchek, who has been on the U.S. coaching staff the last three Olympics.

America's answer to Ian Thorpe

Swimming has become so competitive that many top athletes choose to specialize, but Phelps is so special that he's competitive in many events. He and his coach, Bob Bowman of the North Baltimore Aquatic Club, are zeroing in on which events to focus on for the Athens Games.

Last year, while being ranked first in the world in the 200 fly, Phelps was fourth in both the 200 and 400 IMs. This week at the U.S. championships he'll compete in five events: the 100 and 200 fly, the 200 and 400 IM and the 200 freestyle.

The versatile Phelps has never met the versatile Spitz. He has not seen Spitz's seven gold medal races at the 1972 Olympics.

"I think he has a true appreciation for it," Bowman says. "I don't think he wakes up and says, 'I've got to match Mark Spitz.'"

Phelps relates better to contemporary comparisons, such as the moniker given him for his potential and precociousness: America's answer to Ian Thorpe.

"Being compared to the most dominant swimmer in the world, the best in the world, it's unbelievable," Phelps says.

Thorpe, now 19 and seemingly unbeatable in middle-distance freestyle, won his first world title at 15 — Phelps won his at 16 — and broke his first world record at 16.

"The way they're very different," Bowman says, "is that at 17 years old Michael is a 17-year-old. If you talked to Ian Thorpe at 17, you felt he was much more sophisticated... He's just had a lot more exposure and had to deal with more things."

Bowman's barometer that Phelps is a normal 17-year-old: The kid still breaks into full guffaw while watching movies such as *Dude, Where's My Car?*

Thorpe won three golds and a silver at

Phelps' boyish charm, which is apparent at this August 13, 2000 press conference, is a big part of what makes him so endearing in this age of cocky, pampered multi-millionaire athletes.

the 2000 Olympics in his native Australia, a country that deifies its swimming stars. A millionaire endorser, Thorpe recently came up one silver short of seven gold medals at the Commonwealth Games.

"We've always used Ian a little bit as a yardstick," Bowman says. "Having someone like that who really is light years ahead of everyone else is tremendously motivational. If Michael were the only one, I think it would be hard to keep pushing him."

In Sydney, Phelps was the youngest U.S. male swimmer to compete in the Olympics since 1932. He came away from the only event he swam, the 200 fly, with fifth place — and a scowl. "I think that helped motivate me for six months later breaking the world record. I was not very happy after that swim," Phelps says.

Before the world record, though, there was other business: He got his braces off, and he got his learner's driving permit.

Rare but suitable opportunity

After the world record at the 2001 spring nationals, he got the offer that will alter his life, at least for four years.

A Speedo representative contacted him, wanting to talk about making Phelps the swimsuit manufacturer's youngest male endorser. Swimmers historically have had to wait until they've won some Olympic races to get such an offer.

"Clearly when someone is a world recordholder at age 15 and shows the incredible potential Michael has shown, you immediately have an interest in him," Speedo vice president Stu Isaac says.

Phelps, his coach and his parents debated the pros and cons for months. By signing a contract, he would give up his college eligibility. By foregoing the contract, he would give up the opportunity to train for Athens free of financial worries.

"I'm a firm believer that 99 percent of all

Even as a teenager, Phelps' considerable wingspan and potential were obvious to all who watched him swim.

high school swimmers should swim in college, because that's the next logical step," Bowman says. "It was almost like Michael had already skipped that step. When you have a world record and you're 15, you need to do different things in training and have the freedom to travel and to prepare specifically for the long-course meets without having the other meets interfere."

The Phelps family also knows how tenuous a swimmer's grasp on glory can be. Older sister Whitney was ranked third in the world in the 200 fly at 14. At 15, she was the favorite in the 200 fly at the 1996 Olympic trials. Partly because of a back injury, she finished a shocking sixth. "It definitely scarred our family," Phelps says.

He signed with Speedo in October for a five-figure sum every year until 2005. While Megan Quann also signed with Speedo at 16, no other top U.S. male swimmer has taken this route.

"I'd love to win a national championship, I'd love to win an NCAA title, but the things I'm trying to do right now are bigger than that," Phelps says.

The contract specifically sets aside money for college tuition. Again, Mom insisted. "I said, 'Oh, yes, you are going to college,'" says Debbie, a school administrator in Baltimore County.

Soon Phelps will be folding his wiry frame into the desks at Towson (Md.) High School to study English and economics. He'll be a senior. His swimming accomplishments might get read on the morning announcements. He might sign some autographs in the school hallways. But like anyone else in those hallways, he has his friends to knock him back to reality.

"They always joke when I get beat," Phelps says. "They go, 'Uh, oh, they're going to take your money back now.'"

Sounds like normal 17-year-old stuff. ∾

Early years

Phenomenal Phelps breaks world mark

Leads U.S. team to dominating win over Aussies

By Vicki Michaelis • Date: April 7, 2003

INDIANAPOLIS — Michael Phelps is so precocious in the pool that, at 17, he's already pursuing supernatural standards.

Coming into Sunday's Mutual of Omaha Duel in the Pool, a meet that became a U.S. rout of an understocked Australian team, Phelps wanted to become the first male swimmer to set world records in two different individual events on the same day.

He came up three-hundredths of a second short.

Early in the meet, Phelps beat his own world record in the 400-meter individual medley, winning in 4:10.73. Less than 45 minutes later, the Baltimore native was back in the pool at the sold-out Indiana University Natatorium for the 100 butterfly. He swam a personal-best 51.84 seconds. The world record is 51.81.

"It was a pretty good day," Phelps said. "A few things could have been better."

In the 200 fly Sunday, Phelps overtook 2000 gold medalist Tom Malchow in the last 50 meters for a third victory. Phelps also swam the butterfly leg of the USA's winning medley-relay effort.

"He's great to watch," Australia's Grant Hackett said. "Sometimes I wish he was in my events. He's just an awesome competitor. I love to race people like that."

Hackett was the only Australian to win multiple individual

Soon after he joined the U.S. Olympic team, Phelps began destroying the competition—and threatening world records.

events Sunday. He posted the fastest times ever in a U.S. pool in the 200- meter freestyle and the 1,500 free.

Hackett, unbeaten in the 1,500 since 1997, was Australia's highest-profile entrant. Other top Aussies, such as otherworldly freestyler Ian Thorpe, pulled out recently, citing sickness and other reasons.

The USA had its A team, and the gap made the outcome inevitable. The USA outscored the Aussies 196-74, winning 21 of 26 events and sweeping the top three spots in six. Without Thorpe, and without a close competition, Phelps' pursuit provided the best drama.

"(Saturday) I said this was a test. I think I passed," Phelps said.

Even if he didn't quite get the mark he wanted. ✎

(opposite) Phelps springs off the block on his way to winning the 200-meter individual medley at the U.S. Olympic Team Trials on July 12, 2004. (above) Phelps poses with his father, Fred Phelps, after a press conference.

Early years

Phelps pools his strong points

Focus, intensity, and "perfect build" for world records

By Michael Hiestand • Date: August 6, 2003

BALTIMORE — The hottest teenage athlete in America, for triumphs on a world stage, doesn't have a Nike deal.

But Michael Phelps, 18, doesn't compete in shoes. Or get recognized in public. Or lead an exotic life: "I just play video games, sleep and eat. I'm laid-back. Out of the pool, I'm a normal kid."

In it, he's a tsunami washing over the swimming world.

Phelps, who will compete at the U.S. Summer Nationals this week in College Park, Md., broke five world records at the world championships last month, the first to do that in one meet.

It also positioned him for stardom. At next year's Summer Olympics in Athens, Greece, Phelps will be cast as having a shot at matching Mark Spitz's record seven gold medals in 1972 — or maybe even win an otherworldly eight. Yes, eight.

Rowdy Gaines, who won three Olympic golds in 1984 and will be an NBC analyst at Athens, says it's possible, certainly after Phelps' record world meet. Gaines terms it the greatest performance he has seen in his sport.

Gaines suggests Phelps might compete in five individual events, including butterfly, backstroke and medley, as well as three relays in Athens. And, Gaines says, maybe contend for gold in all. "People might scoff at that, but the scary thing is that's the reality for him."

Phelps is photographed under water following practice at the Meadowbrook Aquatic & Fitness Center in Baltimore, Maryland, where he trains with the North Baltimore Aquatic Club. Phelps had recently returned from the 2003 FINA Swimming World Championships in Barcelona, Spain, where he set five world records.

Room for improvement

Phelps won't predict such success, although he admits he "sort of expected" his unprecedented world meet results. At Athens, he says, he'd face more swimmers specializing in their Olympic events than Spitz did, not to mention he's struggling with a big flaw: "My turns are horrible, probably the slowest on the national team."

Gaines can only laugh: "He has the greatest turns in the world! No question. If he gets any better, I feel pity for everybody else."

Phelps' mother, Deborah, says her son is thinking really big even if he won't say it. "He wants to take his sport to a whole new level," she says.

Phelps, from Towson, Md., outside Baltimore, seems like a natural, with a wingspan longer than his 6' 4" height, unusually long-waisted and kicking with size-14 feet. "He already has the perfect build," Gaines says. "And he's going to get stronger."

Not that Phelps was a late bloomer. "I've seen him ahead of everybody in so many races that this seems like deja vu," his mother says. "But it's wild, because now it's on the world scene."

At 15, Phelps was the youngest U.S. swimmer to qualify for an Olympics when he finished fifth in the 200-meter butterfly at the 2000 Sydney Games. Still 15, he became the youngest man, in 2001, to break a world record, the 200 butterfly. At 16, he became the youngest U.S. swimmer to turn pro.

It helped that Phelps grew up training with the North Baltimore Aquatic Club, which has produced several Olympians. The club even requires its grade-school racers to wear Athens 2004 swim caps. Bob Bowman, who coaches 18 elite swimmers, including Phelps, figures about a dozen will go to the U.S. Olympic trials.

And Phelps' older sisters, Hilary and Whitney, also raced and gave their brother an early opportunity to see the pressures. Whitney made the U.S. team at 14 and was a favorite to qualify for the 200 butterfly for the 1996 Atlanta Olympics. Michael, then 10 and known as "Little Phelps," watched her miss the cut in her qualifying. "That was really hard on the family," he says.

His mother "didn't want a repeat of 1996" when he tried to qualify for Sydney. Whitney was the first person to hug him when he made it.

But Phelps' true strength might be his single-mindedness, which flies in the face of what one of his grade-school teachers once told his mother: that her energetic son wouldn't "ever have the ability to focus on anything in life."

The teacher hadn't seen him swim.

"I don't know why he has such intensity," Bowman says. "He always relishes the opportunity to compete. He's never uncomfortable. He can block out every distraction."

Kevin Clements, 23, who trains with Phelps and competed at worlds in the 200

individual medley, admires Phelps' prerace focus: "He just pushes everybody out and concentrates on himself."

Phelps says he'll often pick a song and sing it over and over to himself to get through hours of practice. Before races, he relies on headphones.

"Listening to music puts me in my own zone, it blocks everything out," he says. Music from rapper Eminem, he says, is particularly effective.

No dogging it from here

Don Talbot, a veteran coach for the powerful Australian swimmers, made a big mistake in suggesting Phelps was unproven before July's world meet in Barcelona. There, as one Australian paper put it, Phelps was a "a one-man wrecking crew to Australia's pride."

It wasn't a coincidence. "It multiplied (my motivation) by 10," Phelps says. "Anything negative fires me up."

His other motivations are more idiosyncratic. His mother allows him to use his endorsement earnings after world records for rewards such as the special rims he bought for his Cadillac SUV.

Before the world meet, her son asked for a dog "that will lick my face and sleep with me." At worlds, she signaled him by holding up her fingers. "People thought that was about world records. But it meant one dog, two dogs, then a whole litter!"

Her son doesn't have one yet. But Phelps is adamant about a quest that might result in more records falling: "I can't decide whether I want a Lab or a little dog. But I've always wanted a dog." ❧

Phelps stays immersed in music right up until he plunges into the pool for a race.

Early years

Let the Phelps gold rush begin

USA's versatile swimmer starts trail from trials to Athens, possible glory

By Vicki Michaelis • Date: July 7, 2004

LONG BEACH — Michael Phelps, already anointed the USA's cover boy of the Athens Olympics, can't imagine there is anything more people want to know about him.

"Everything's out there. There's nothing to hide," says the 19-year-old swimmer, with Mark Spitz-like medal potential.

Yet until last week, Phelps was holding back on something that had the swimming world abuzz. Whenever asked what events he would swim at the U.S. Olympic trials, which begin today in Long Beach, he answered only with a sly smile.

That the question even needed to be asked points to the reason a teenager from suburban Baltimore who does little more than eat, sleep, swim and recite lines from the movie *Tommy Boy* has our attention.

He is a rare Renaissance man in the water. So versatile is his talent that Phelps had the luxury of waiting, evaluating, then choosing only the events at the Olympic trials that give him the chance to be a world-beater.

"There's versatility, and then there's versatility at the top level," says Eddie Reese, the U.S. Olympic men's swimming coach. "That just doesn't happen."

Phelps' pursuit of Spitz's 1972 record of seven gold medals,

Phelps constantly fine-tunes his preparation for events with longtime coach Bob Bowman, as he does in this August 2000 photo.

and the $1 million bonus he'll get from swimming apparel sponsor Speedo if he makes it happen, starts today with the 400-meter individual medley.

"I have a feeling of empathy," Spitz says. "I hope he does (win seven golds). It doesn't take away a thing that I have accomplished."

Phelps' results between now and Tuesday, when he's scheduled to swim the last of the six events he has entered at the trials, will show whether the multiple-medal projections are more lock or long shot and whether the media blitz is more justified hype or misplaced hope.

"I've made my goal public, and my goal is to win one Olympic medal," Phelps says. The media "are putting the seven gold medals out there. One will not be a failure to me."

Phelps' trials plan went public last week when USA Swimming posted the entry lists on its Web site. He is entered in the 200-and 400-meter individual medleys, the 100 and 200 butterfly, the 200 backstroke and the 200 freestyle.

He probably needs to win five individual events at the Olympics to reach the Spitz standard. The other two golds would come from relays.

In Spitz's time, the U.S. men ruled the relays, giving team members three nearly guaranteed gold medals. Now, the USA must deal with countries such as Australia, which broke the Americans' unbeaten record in the 400 free relay in Sydney.

Spitz won his seven golds (four individual) relying on the freestyle and the butterfly. Matt Biondi, who stirred Spitz fever going into the 1988 Olympics, also competed in just the freestyle and butterfly. Biondi won five gold medals, a silver and a bronze in '88.

Phelps' repertoire is built on the IM, an event that combines all four strokes and allows for a training regimen that lends itself to versatility.

"It's just amazing. It just seems like he could do anything," says Tracy Caulkins, who once held U.S. records and titles in all four swim strokes — the freestyle, breaststroke, backstroke and butterfly — and was favored to win at least five medals at the 1980 Olympics before the USA boycotted those Games. "I don't think I was as competitive across the board."

Phelps says jokingly, "I could win 15 gold medals if I wanted to."

U.S. trials could pose biggest test

Phelps is the reigning world champion in three of the events he plans to swim at the trials (the 200 and 400 IMs and the 200 fly) and was ranked second in the world last year in the other three.

Except for the 200 free, an event ruled by Australian uber-swimmer Ian Thorpe in recent years, Phelps will get a taste of his toughest competition at the trials, where

---

Phelps waves to the crowd after a medal ceremony at the Long Beach Swim Stadium in Long Beach, California on July 7, 2004. He won the 400-meter individual medley in world-record time of 4:08.41.

only the top two finishers in each event qualify for the Olympics.

Over seven days at the trials, Phelps is expected to swim 17 events. His toughest challenges will come in his final days. Sunday, Phelps will have heats in the 200 back and 200 IM in the morning, then the 200 back semifinals and 200 IM semifinal at night. The next night, he'll swim the 200 back finals, 200 IM finals and 100 fly semifinal.

Monday's 200 back finals and Tuesday's 100 fly finals will be the most anticipated races.

In the 200 back, U.S. teammate Aaron Peirsol is the reigning world champion. He beat Phelps at that distance and in the 100 back at a meet in May.

In the 100 fly, Phelps will try to beat the USA's Ian Crocker, who edged Phelps for the 2003 world title in a race in which they both beat the then-world record.

"I'm still doing my normal thing either way," he says. "I'm going to go into trials first and do what I can to swim as fast as I can swim. After that, whatever happens happens."

At last year's world championships, Phelps broke five world records and won four gold medals. At the 2003 summer nationals, he won five national titles.

He became the youngest man to break a world record when he did it in the 200 fly at 15 years, 9 months. He finished fifth at the 2000 Olympics in the 200 fly, the only event he swam at the Sydney Games.

Phelps has six national and two world titles in the butterfly, 20 national and four world titles overall.

Mapping out precise strategy

The preparation for an Olympic program that could have Phelps swimming a semifinal event in one stroke and the finals in another stroke the same night is a long-term commitment.

"This isn't just a four-year process. It's a 10-year process," says Bob Bowman, his coach of eight years.

Bowman precisely calibrates the time spent on each stroke, as well as the intensity and distance of Phelps' training swims to build speed and endurance.

In the last two years, Phelps has focused on the breaststroke and backstroke for part of the year and the freestyle and butterfly the other part, although he still works on every stroke every week.

Phelps not only swims varied strokes but also competes at different distances. The 100-meter events require the speed of a sprinter. The 400-meter events require the endurance of a distance swimmer.

During an endurance-building phase, which sometimes lasts up to 30 weeks, Phelps will swim at least 80,000 meters (49.7 miles) a week. That includes some double-session days that have him swimming 16,000 meters (9.9 miles). For a speed-work phase, the distance is reduced to 60,000 meters (37.3 miles) a week, with

600-800 meters a day at race pace.

Although Phelps could keep his options somewhat flexible going into the Olympic trials, he and Bowman had a framework in mind all along. Over the past year, they kept an eye on the times other top swimmers were posting and how Phelps was doing in head-to-head races, although Bowman says that didn't figure heavily into the program.

"I can quite honestly say (the trials plan) is the same today as it was in August of last year," right after the world championships, Bowman says. The plan, however, still could change over the next week.

"If a particular stroke is doing really well or another is not doing well, we would have to take that into account — and we still may," Bowman says.

Trials competitors can drop events during the meet but cannot add any. The schedule is working in Phelps' favor because his performance today in the 400 IM will allow him and Bowman to evaluate his strokes before deciding to alter or stick to his program.

Other U.S. swimmers, including Peirsol, have expressed some irritation over Phelps' secrecy. His guardedness kept everyone guessing as to who would have to contend with him.

"That kind of keeps the pressure off of Michael and keeps the pressure on his competitors," says Mark Schubert, the U.S. Olympic women's coach. "There was no reason for him to talk about his plan. He could keep it to himself and follow it. That way, he keeps to a minimum the speculation and the potential criticism."

That way, all he had to worry about in going into these trials was eating, sleeping, swimming and working on his impression of the *Tommy Boy* line that could come in handy if he finds himself wearing seven gold medals in Athens:

"I've seen some crazy stuff in my time, but that . . . was . . . awesome!" ৵

Phelps practices a turn at the Meadowbrook Aquatic & Fitness Center in Baltimore, fresh off the 2003 FINA Swimming World Championships in Barcelona, Spain, where he set five world records.

Medals, history weigh heavily upon Phelps

Quest for seven gold medals a daunting task

By Christine Brennan • Date: July 8, 2004

LONG BEACH — No matter how dedicated the swimmer, no matter how focused and driven, it is impossible to block out the siren song of trying to win seven Olympic gold medals. The swimmer can tell himself it's pure folly, nothing but a setup for a huge fall, yet he cannot ignore the call. Seven golds is 755 home runs. It's 17-0. It's Mark Spitz. It's magic.

Two consecutive generations now have given us a swimmer who wanted to reach seven golds, who wanted to be Spitz. In 1988, Matt Biondi went to Seoul hoping to match Spitz. He won five gold medals, one silver and one bronze. Winning five golds was a stunning achievement, except for the fact that millions of sports fans thought he was going to win seven. His five golds required a disclaimer. Sadly, Biondi became something of an Olympic disappointment. All because he tried for seven.

Now Michael Phelps, who set a world record to win his first event at the Olympic trials Wednesday, is attempting the quest. He is going about it quite casually, with a slouch and a sleepy shrug, the way you'd expect a gangly 19-year-old who still lives at home with his mother to attack almost any goal, including cleaning his room.

He has never met Spitz and doesn't seem very excited to do so. He speaks of a vague notion of taking the sport of swim-

Phelps didn't ask for the scrutiny, but it came with his prolific performances. As much as any athlete in the history of any sport, Phelps has risen to the occasion time and again.

45

ming to "a new level," although one wonders how that's ever going to happen on the jam-packed American sports television landscape. Especially in an endeavor that attracts serious interest only once every four years and in which the personalities spend much of their time with their heads under water.

On occasion, Phelps even acts altogether blase about all this talk of seven gold medals, saying winning just one is his goal, although that seems disingenuous. He has already fallen into that bad habit athletes have of blaming the media for anything and everything. He told USA TODAY's Vicki Michaelis that the media "are putting the seven gold medals out there. One will not be a failure to me."

Unfortunately, he's wrong on both counts. The truth of the Phelps quest is that it's his sponsors who are fervently fanning the flames in every announcement they make. The media are only following the lead of Speedo, which, in an unabashed publicity stunt, has offered Phelps $1 million if he matches Spitz's seven gold medals in Athens.

And it's not just Speedo. The Omega watch people sent out a press release Wednesday saying none other than super-model Cindy Crawford will "induct" Phelps into the "Omega family of brand ambassadors" next week. "Expectations are that he will capture more medals than the legendary Mark Spitz," exclaimed the breathless press release.

With pressure like this, who needs opponents?

"I have to say I'm not envious of his position," said veteran Olympian Jenny Thompson, who went into the 1992 Barcelona Games with expectations to win five gold medals, but won only two, both in the relays.

Another mistake Phelps made was to say it would not be a failure if he wins just one gold. For himself, internally, perhaps it would

be acceptable. But for his sponsors, and the public's perception of him, it would be devastating. It sounds like it's time for Phelps' agent and the PR folks at Speedo and Omega to come clean with their client and tell him about the flip side of fame.

Phelps' story is the dilemma of the Olympian in search of the big payoff. With a window of opportunity that is no more than a few months wide, Phelps had no choice but to set himself up like this; if he had said he was going to try to win, say, three Olympic gold medals, no one would have paid any special attention to him. And most major corporations wouldn't have given him the time of day.

"The opportunity for an athlete after having success at the Olympics is very small," said veteran backstroker Lenny Krayzelburg, the winner of three gold medals at the 2000 Olympics. "Fortunately or unfortunately, he'll be judged by the Olympic Games. There's no question (not winning all seven golds) could be disappointing."

This is not going to be an easy task for Phelps. Specialists will be gunning for him when he enters their event.

"It's important to know there are other swimmers in the meet," said world champion Aaron Peirsol, who will race Phelps in the 200 backstroke.

What's more, three of Spitz's gold medals came in relays, which were a gimme for the American men back in 1972. That's not the case this time for the U.S. team, or Phelps.

"I'm not going to count him out, but it's a real lofty goal," said Tom Malchow, who won the 2000 Olympic gold medal in the 200 butterfly, another of Phelps' races. "He's carrying the weight of the sport on his shoulders. People still talk about Spitz today, but that's a lot of hope to put on a 19-year-old." ❧

With the spotlight comes commercial opportunity, and Phelps has earned considerable gold outside the pool as well.

After trials of few errors, Phelps faces real test

Pursuit of seven golds at Athens full of pitfalls

By Vicki Michaelis • Date: July 14, 2004

LONG BEACH — Michael Phelps did much more than dip his toe in the water to test his lofty Olympic ambitions at the U.S. swimming trials.

In seven days, he qualified for six individual Olympic events, more than any U.S. swimmer in history. He competed in six finals and won four. He stepped on the starting block 17 times, one day doing so four times in little more than an hour.

He felt the cold splash of a competitor's victory celebration and came back for more.

He broke one of his own world records. He saw world-record swims twice nick his invincibility. He filled the stands and made headlines and the nightly news for an oft-over-looked sport.

Starting Aug. 14 in Athens, the 19-year-old from suburban Baltimore will do it all again, on a bigger stage against tougher competition with weightier expectations.

"Nothing I do over there will be easy," Phelps says. "I knew that before I got into this. Off of this performance we can change some things and work on some things in the next five weeks, and hopefully I'll be in better shape."

For Phelps, the U.S. trials were about more than making the Olympic team. They were his own personal preliminaries in a head-to-head with swimming history. Phelps has Mark

Phelps qualified for six individual events at the Athens Olympic trials. By also swimming in two relays, Phelps was eyeing a potential eight gold medals.

Michael Phelps: The World's Greatest Olympian

Spitz's 1972 Olympic record medal haul of seven golds in his sights.

"Michael is a phenomenal swimmer, and he's trying to do something really special," says Ian Crocker, who broke his own world record to beat Phelps in the 100-meter butterfly Tuesday. "He's attracting attention to this sport that we haven't had in a long time, and it's a healthy thing. And I'm really glad that it's happening."

Pinpointing the challenges

Whether Spitz-like magic can happen in Athens depends on Phelps' ability to mount an answer to the challenge laid before him this week. A day before Crocker edged him in the 100 fly, Aaron Peirsol beat him in the 200 backstroke, also in world-record time.

"We'll have to see how things play out in Athens," Phelps says. "I'm not going to say there is going to be a different outcome, but it's a possibility."

Phelps posted a magazine cover of Crocker in his bedroom after Crocker beat him in last year's world championships. As Phelps prepares over the next five weeks, he likely will wake up to images of not only Crocker and Peirsol but also Australian all-world freestyler Ian Thorpe, who awaits in the 200 free if Phelps swims that event.

Of the three races — the 100 fly, 200 back and 200 free — Phelps will have to win at least one for a shot at seven golds. He might have to win more than one if the USA doesn't overcome its underdog status in two of the three relays or if he falters in any of his other three individual events. He will be heavily favored in the 200 and 400 individual medleys and the 200 fly, as he's the world record-holder in each.

"I think he can be better than he was (at the trials)," says Phelps' coach, Bob Bowman. "But there are a lot of fast people out there."

Pending a decision on whether he'll compete in all six individual events for which he qualified, Phelps' Olympic schedule will mirror the one he had at the trials and add relays. It's a schedule he and Bowman began calibrating last year, the moment they had the days and times of the Athens swimming events.

If he competes in all six individual events, Phelps will start out with one of his strongest events, the 400 individual medley. He opened the trials by beating his own world mark.

After the 400 IM, the Olympic schedule, like the one at the trials, allows Phelps to alternate his stronger individual events with those in which he faces more formidable obstacles, giving him a built-in cushion for mental and physical recovery.

The busiest night of the schedule, for example, has him opening with the 200 back but following with the 200 IM final.

Phelps rebounded from the loss to Peirsol on Monday well enough to win the 200 IM in 1:56.71 less than 30 minutes later. Phelps, who swam the first 100 of the IM race under

---

Phelps began calibrating his schedule for Athens as soon as the Olympics event schedule was published, one year prior to the Games.

the world-record pace, finished more than two seconds faster than second-place Ryan Lochte and less than eight-tenths of a second slower than his own world record.

"After the 200 back, he was not pleased," Bowman says. "He likes to win. But he immediately channeled that into energy for the next one, which was really, I thought, remarkable."

Short-term thinking pays off

At the Olympics, Phelps will be tested more stringently than Spitz was because of the addition since 1972 of semifinals in 200-meter races. Spitz swam 13 times in 1972. Phelps could swim up to 20 times.

"When I was swimming every single day," Spitz says, "I realized the most important part of my program was that I had to constantly forget about what I just did and think about what I had to do for the next day."

Phelps doesn't see it as a test as much as a habit. Thoughts of whatever event he just swam can be chased away in the amount of time it takes to cue the next piece of rap music on his portable player.

"I've been doing it all my life," Phelps says. "It's my everyday routine when it comes to a meet."

In Athens, the race pace and competition will be anything but everyday. Phelps won the 200 free at the trials in 1:46.27, more than two seconds slower than Thorpe's world record in the event. Thorpe is not the only competitor Phelps would have to vanquish at the Olympics: the Netherlands' Pieter van den Hoogenband, who beat Thorpe in the 200 free in the Sydney Games, will be a factor.

"Having to swim against very top-caliber swimmers in the world in these events at a meet of this level is the challenge," says Bowman, who adds that having to race swimmers who specialize in one or two strokes is the "biggest hurdle."

Complicating any equation that adds to seven golds — a total that would pay Phelps a $1 million bonus from swimming apparel sponsor Speedo — is the relays.

In Spitz's time, the USA was a lock to win relays. In 1972, the U.S. team, using reserves, set a world record in the qualifying round of the 4x100-meter freestyle relay. The team that included Spitz eclipsed that record in the finals, winning the race by more than three seconds.

Australia broke the USA's unbeaten streak in Olympic 400 free relays in 2000. The USA hasn't won the 400 free relay since. Australia also topped the USA in the 4x200-meter freestyle relay in Sydney.

Whatever he must do to mine seven Olympic golds, Phelps doesn't spend a lot of time doing the math. He just keeps swimming, lap after practice lap, race after big race. History is at the far wall.

"Spitz did it," Phelps says, "so obviously it is possible." ❧

At 19 years old, Phelps was carrying the expectations of a nation on his broad shoulders as the U.S. prepared for the 2004 Olympics in Athens, Greece.

Phelps in fast lane for a record engagement

Olympian has big ambitions, little-boy charm

By Vicki Michaelis • Date: August 13, 2004

As spring rounded into the biggest summer of his 19-year-old life, Michael Phelps took a photo with his cellphone of what he really wants. That way he could see it at the touch of a keypad. He could show it around, hear the oohs and aahs.

An Olympic gold medal? No. Seven Olympic gold medals? Guess again.

"It's a one-month-old English bulldog," he says after pulling up the photo with the grinning expectancy of a child in a toy store aisle. "I love bulldogs. It's a big dog, but it's a little dog, too. You know what I mean?"

Phelps is the big dog of the USA's 2004 Olympic team. Entered in five individual swimming events and eligible for three relays, the protean prodigy from suburban Baltimore could stamp Olympic history with his size 14 feet and size XXXL potential by matching or surpassing Mark Spitz's seven gold medals. Eight medals of any color would give Phelps the most of any Olympian in a non-boycotted Games.

"Mark was truly incredible," U.S. Olympic men's coach Eddie Reese says of Spitz. "Michael Phelps is beyond that."

"Little Phelps"

Yet Phelps is not far removed from the kid dubbed "Little Phelps" when he played by the pool deck and later swam in the same club as his two older sisters.

Phelps and Bowman discuss strategy before a training race in August 2004.

Phelps lives at home with his mom. He plays video games and poker with friends he has had since elementary school. He loves his car, a Cadillac Escalade (a photo of that also is on his cellphone).

"I'm delighted to say he hasn't changed," says Bob Bowman, his coach of eight years.

Oldest sister Hilary, now 26, earned a swimming scholarship at the University of Richmond. Whitney, 24, swam at UNLV and came up achingly short of making the 1996 Olympic team.

"Little Phelps" became the youngest man ever to set a world swimming record (at 15 years, 9 months), the youngest U.S. male swimmer to turn professional (at 16), and the only swimmer to break five world records in one international meet (the 2003 worlds) and to qualify for the Olympics in six individual events.

Phelps was born about the time his family discovered its propensity for the pool. On a pediatrician's advice, his mom had enrolled Hilary and Whitney in swimming lessons. They were starting to compete when Michael arrived.

"I remember taking him out of his crib, putting him in the car and driving to practice or a competition. He grew up around the pool," says his mom, Debbie, an administrator for Baltimore County schools.

His first brush with Olympic disappointment came in the 1996 trials, where Whitney, a favorite in the 200 butterfly, finished sixth while feeling the first symptoms of chronic back problems that would prematurely end her career.

Whitney was on the pool deck to congratulate her brother when, at 15, he qualified in the 200 fly for the 2000 Olympics, where he finished fifth. He was the youngest man on the U.S. Olympic swimming team since 1932.

"It was so unbelievable because he went from this little kid to all of a sudden making the Olympic team," Whitney says. "I was like, 'What happened to the in-between stage?'"

Out of the pool, he's still in it. He called his mom in May from a pet store, begging her to guess what he had in his arms, then asking if he could bring the bulldog puppy home.

"The word 'no' never rolled off my tongue," his mom says. "I just said, 'If you bring the dog home' . . . and then I went through a whole list of things he had to have."

At the top of the list was time at home, and for Phelps, that's in short supply right now.

Pre-Games hype

Phelps' sprint to the crest of his sport, combined with artful marketing, has him enjoying the kind of fame and fortune — and the demands that come — that Olympians usually don't realize until after they've stood on the medal stand.

He already has done *The Tonight Show*. He's a multimillionaire with endorsements ranging from Speedo to AT&T Wireless to Visa. Speedo will give him another $1 million

Phelps stretches before the 200-meter individual medley at the U.S. Olympic Trials.

if he wins seven golds.

His image peppers newsstands and commercials. Bowman interjects while glancing at a television during a phone interview: "Michael's on NBC. All Michael, all the time — that's my life right now."

Bowman foresaw this when, at age 11, Phelps set an age-group national record in the 100-meter butterfly. Bowman talked to Phelps' parents about his potential, suggesting the Olympics were within reach if his athletic focus became singular. Phelps, also playing baseball and lacrosse at the time, initially resisted.

Once he set in his mind to make it happen, his body followed. Now 6' 4", he has a torso that if it were any longer would make him appear as if in a fun-house mirror, with a wingspan capable of bear-hugging his Escalade.

Phelps' physical dimensions give him uncommon command and versatility in the water. The individual medley, which incorporates all four swim strokes, is his signature event.

His mental ability to handle enormous expectation with aplomb and a simple phrase, "Whatever happens, happens," has been just as instrumental in shaping him as a swimmer, Bowman says.

"I don't know what goes on in there," Bowman says of Phelps' mind, "but I like it."

Phelps responds even to difficult questions — some of the toughest are about his distanced relationship with his father, Fred — with typical teenager cool. Phelps' parents divorced when he was 7.

"We'll throw e-mails back and forth every now and then," he says of his dad. "But the way it has been over the past few years is it's been the same. So going into this year, I'd rather just keep everything the same, keep things normal, just go with the flow."

Underneath the mellow surface is a competitor Bowman can roil merely by mentioning a competitor's quote from a newspaper article. When U.S. teammate Ian Crocker pinned him with his only individual loss in the 2003 worlds, Phelps posted a photo of Crocker in his bedroom.

"He's very loud when he loses," says Matt Townsend, Phelps' best friend since fourth grade. "When something doesn't go his way, he's very, very, very verbal. He has like a win addiction, I would say. If he loses, he'll say, 'Let's go best two out of three or best three out of five.'"

Starting Saturday, "Little Phelps" has up to eight chances over eight days to become the Olympics' all-time big dog. Whether or not it happens, look for a few additions to the cellphone photo album.

"I like the Escalade," Phelps says, "but I want a sedan, like a big car. I definitely want to get the dog. That's definitely coming after this year.

"It's not a problem finding things that I want."

Or, it seems, finding a way to get them. ❧

Peter Vanderkaay, Phelps, and Ryan Lochte celebrate after setting an American team record. Anchor leg swimmer Klete Keller is not pictured

Phelps remains golden boy despite bronze

Baltimore's favorite son still a hero in his hometown

By Amy Rosewater • Date: August 16, 2004

BALTIMORE — Lou Sharkey heard the news when he received a phone call while he was driving Sunday: Michael Phelps' quest for eight Olympic gold medals was over. Phelps and his American teammates placed third in the 4x100 freestyle relay.

"No," Sharkey said. "Really? Oh man."

Not a second later, Sharkey recovered from the shock.

"Well, it's still a bronze," he said. "You can't win them all."

Sharkey knows Phelps well. For the past five years, Sharkey has cooked up a massive daily breakfast, complete with eggs and chocolate chip pancakes, for Phelps at his restaurant, Pete's Grill, in the Baltimore neighborhood of Waverly. Even though Phelps won't be able to surpass Mark Spitz's record of seven Olympic golds, Sharkey remains proud of his buddy.

"Am I proud of him?" Sharkey said. "Oh my God, yeah. Nobody can live up to that hype. He gave everyone something to look forward to, and he already got one gold medal. He could not win another one, and we'll still be proud of him.

"I told him months and months ago, long before anyone else knew about going for eight events, that he shouldn't try to live up to everyone else. I told him, 'Win one,' and that's more than most everyone else does in a lifetime."

Many of the regular customers at Pete's Grill have met

Phelps and Jason Lezak pose with their bronze medals after the 4x100-meter relay final at the Olympic Aquatic Center.

Phelps and have become fans. He is hugely popular in Baltimore, and his achievements have been well documented in the local media. Although local fans are proud of his swimming ability, he has become even more endearing for his likeable personality and low-key attitude. No matter how he fares in Athens, many locals said, they will remain fans.

"I see him in here," said Terry Duncan-Ross, after eating a Belgian waffle, bacon and coffee. "He'll sit and answer questions when people ask them. He is no superstar, though. He's very level-headed. People come in here to eat. I'm not even sure a lot of people know who he is when he's here."

Another customer, Michael Gisriel, said he hoped Phelps would win "at least five" golds.

"Five would be good," Gisriel said. "I hope he does that. It's a lot. In the old days, the relays weren't as competitive. Now, they are."

Sharkey, who spoke briefly with Phelps after his gold medal performance in the 400 IM Saturday, said he plans on having a meal with him when Phelps returns: a big breakfast for a champion.

Outside of Sharkey's restaurant is a banner that reads: "Good Luck Mike. Go For The Gold."

About 10 minutes away, another Phelps banner is hanging outside of Ryan's Daughter, an Irish brewpub in Baltimore's Belvedere Square. Owner Donal Doyle has hosted nightly Olympic parties in honor of Phelps and the North Baltimore Aquatic Club, Phelps' swim team.

The partying won't stop just because Phelps' Olympic quest for eight golds is over.

On Saturday night, when NBC broadcast Phelps' gold medal swim, more than 200 fans turned out at Doyle's restaurant to cheer. Debbie Phelps, Michael's mother, donated some of her son's swimming gear as door prizes.

Tonight, many of those same fans will be back at Ryan's Daughter.

"Frankly, I'm kind of glad the pressure is off of him now" said John Cadigan, who manages the Meadowbrook pool. "He's got his one gold medal, and now he can focus."

Whether Phelps returns to Baltimore with one gold or more, Cadigan will be proud of Meadowbrook's most famous swimmer.

"He's a once-in-a-generation swimmer," Cadigan says.

"He certainly shows the rest of the world what we've been seeing for years." ❧

Phelps and Takashi Yamamoto of Japan show off their gold and silver medals from the 200-meter butterfly finals.

Phelps' big win: Taking challenge

Deserves applause for taking a shot at history

By Christine Brennan • Date: August 17, 2004

ATHENS — The big race has given us the big letdown. Michael Phelps has lost. Mark Spitz is safe. You all are free to start paying attention to gymnastics now.

That hissing sound you hear is the air being let out of the most hyped story coming into these Olympic Games. Phelps, the 19-year-old so full of hope heading into his eight events here, was left muttering about how "emotionally draining" these Olympics already have been after winning his second consecutive bronze medal at the swimming venue. He now has one gold medal and two bronze medals, with five events left to go.

"It's definitely a whole lot different from (the U.S.) trials," a subdued Phelps said after finding out just how difficult it is to beat the Thorpedo, Ian Thorpe, in one of the Australian's beloved events, the 200 freestyle. "It takes a lot out of you, race to race."

Now that Phelps cannot reach Spitz's seven gold medals, the most compelling question left at the swimming venue is exactly how America — from Peoria to Madison Avenue — will view his performance at these Olympics. His sponsors and his agent took a calculated risk, trying to attach themselves to Spitz in a quest that was all but impossible from the get-go.

But now that Phelps and seven golds have been inextricably linked for weeks by his publicity-seeking sponsors — and in countless covers and headlines splashed around the world — how does Phelps escape the mantle that has awaited others

Despite earning two bronze medals and just one gold in his first three events, Phelps would rally for many more golden memories in Athens.

who have failed to reach Spitz, the terrible label of "disappointment?"

Whatever Phelps' medal haul becomes — from his one certain gold to the possibility of a magnificent six — there will be those who think of seven and do the math. It happened to Matt Biondi in 1988, when he entered seven events in Seoul and came away with five golds, one silver and one bronze. It will happen to Phelps here. It's simply the nature of great expectations in sports in America.

The buildup to the 200 freestyle, the ultimate Olympic battle, was like that of a title fight. Saturday night, the first day of swimming at these Games, was a majestic display of two sportsmen reveling in the moment — and also jockeying for position with Monday very much on their minds.

Less than a half-hour after Phelps won his first gold medal in the 400 individual medley, Thorpe won his in the 400 freestyle. Organizers might as well have played "Anything you can do, I can do better . . . " over the public-address system.

They held separate interviews, but it was as if they were linked in everything they did. They were asked what they thought about each other. They looked ahead to racing each other in 48 hours. They were two men inexorably moving toward a place and time that both wanted to call their own.

Phelps, two years Thorpe's junior, acted differently than he did even a month ago. In July at the U.S. trials, he was the gangly teenager next door, the young man still living with his mother, whiling away the days eating, sleeping and swimming.

By Saturday night, he had been transformed into some kind of Coubertinian creation. When he and the second-place finisher, who happened to be his American teammate, Erik Vendt, came together in the pool after the race, it was Phelps who lifted Vendt's arm in triumph, not vice versa.

"This is a dream come true to me," Phelps said. "But it means even more with Erik winning the silver medal." Maybe it's just me, but I have trouble imagining some of the multimillionaire U.S. men's basketball players being as respectful of a vanquished foe.

With so much talk of Spitz's seven golds, Phelps for the first time sounded genuinely thrilled with just one. "My goal is right here," he said, tugging on the gold medal. "I'm perfectly happy right now."

Phelps didn't even have to swim the 200 freestyle, which is not his best event, not at all. He didn't have to accept this challenge, and yet he did. He could have taken the easy route and avoided Thorpe. But he chose not to. "One of the things I've wanted to do," Phelps said, "is to race Thorpe in a freestyle event before either one of us is done."

Who knew athletes talked like this anymore? What kind of medal do you hand an athlete who simply wants to test himself? And, in defeat, isn't he also some kind of winner? ✎

Phelps tunes out the distractions as he stretches before a morning training session at the Olympic Aquatic Center.

Eight medals later, Phelps eyes his future

What he will do for an encore is anyone's guess

By Vicki Michaelis • Date: August 24, 2004

ATHENS — Michael Phelps won so many gold medals he wasn't sure which one he was wearing at a news conference Sunday.

"I can't read Greek," he said when asked. "It's one of the 200s."

That would be the 200-meter butterfly or the 200 individual medley, two of the four individual races Phelps won. He also won gold in two relays and bronze in two other races for a total of eight, the most for anyone at a non-boycotted Olympics.

Phelps plans to stay in Athens through the closing ceremonies to see some other events and spend some downtime with his family at the Games. But the 19-year-old is eager to get back to the suburban Baltimore house where he lives with his mom. "I miss going to breakfast at Pete's (the diner near his practice pool where he eats almost daily). I miss my car. I miss the house. I miss my cat. I miss everything at home," Phelps said.

Phelps' next competition is the World Championships on Oct. 7-11 in Indianapolis.

Sometime before the end of the year, Phelps will move to Ann Arbor, Mich. His coach, Bob Bowman, has been hired as the University of Michigan swimming coach.

As a professional athlete with multimillion-dollar endorsements, Phelps can't swim for the Wolverines. But he can train with them. He also will enroll at the university, with an eye toward majoring in "something in sports —

Phelps cheers on teammates during the finals of Olympic swimming competition in August 2004.

sports marketing or sports business."

He hasn't been in the pool since Friday, when he beat U.S. teammate Ian Crocker in the 100 fly by 0.04 seconds. Soon after the race, Phelps decided to concede the spot in Saturday's 4x100 medley relay he had earned with the victory to Crocker. Phelps' reason was twofold: He said Crocker's relay takeoffs are better, and that he wanted Crocker — who was slowed by a sore throat when he led off the 4x100 freestyle relay to a disappointing bronze finish earlier in the week — to have another chance at a relay gold.

With Crocker swimming the fly leg, the U.S. men won the medley relay in world-record time.

The gold medal counts toward Phelps' total because Phelps swam the fly leg in the preliminaries.

Although Phelps matched Soviet gymnast Alexander Dityatin's medal total (Dityatin won eight in the 1980 Olympics, which were boycotted by the USA and more than 50 other countries), he was one gold short of matching Mark Spitz's record medal haul in 1972.

The $1 million bonus Speedo would've paid Phelps to meet the Spitz mark also is payable at the '08 Games. Asked if he'd embark on the quest again, Phelps said, "I wouldn't count anything out." ✎

(opposite) Phelps cheers the 4x100 medley relay team as they swim to a gold medal in world record time of 3:30.68. (above) The medalists in the men's 200-meter freestyle (left to right), Michael Phelps of the USA (bronze) and Ian Thorpe of Australia (gold), show off their medals for photographers at the Olympic Aquatic Center.

Evolving Phelps not just treading water

World event is test to find what needs work for Beijing

By Vicki Michaelis • Date: July 19, 2005

This time, it's not about the gold.

At the world swimming championships, which start Sunday in Montreal, Michael Phelps aims to take nothing more than "baby steps."

"I just want to go in and race, to find little things I can work on and improve," Phelps says.

Phelps' trophy haul at last year's Summer Olympics was no little thing. He won eight medals, six gold, leaving Athens the most decorated athlete of a non-boycotted Games.

But he'll dive back into highly competitive waters at Montreal a work in progress. Just as his arrest on a DUI charge in November reminded everyone — above all, the 20-year-old Phelps — that he's still growing as a person, his plan for Montreal shows he still is developing as a swimmer.

"I'm still learning about swimming, 12 years into it," he says.

Phelps has not backed off his ambitious program. He intends to swim in five individual events and three relays, as he did in Athens.

But he has dropped two of the events he dominates most, the 400-meter individual medley and 200-meter butterfly, to make room in his packed schedule for the 100- and 400-meter freestyles, where he will be an underdog.

Phelps' fearsome finishing kick gives U.S. teammate Jason

Phelps, winner of the 100-meter backstroke, catches his breath immediately after the event. He missed setting a world record by .03 second at the 2007 U.S. swimming national championships in August 2007.

Lezak and South Africans Roland Schoeman and Ryk Neethling a reason to start strong and keep their distance in the 100, but a Phelps win would be a significant upset. Australian Grant Hackett's best time this year in the 400 is more than three seconds faster than Phelps'.

"A lot of the international guys are taking a step back," says Dave Salo, U.S. men's coach for worlds. He notes that Australia's Ian Thorpe and the Netherlands' Pieter van den Hoogenband — the only swimmers to beat Phelps in an individual event in Athens — won't be in Montreal. "But Michael's a pretty focused, determined individual."

For Phelps this is about a much longer race, one that ends at the 2008 Summer Games in Beijing. Experience in the 100 makes him a stronger teammate in the 400 free relay, an event the USA hasn't won for five years. The 400 forces him to work on his freestyle stroke and his pacing for distance events.

In an approach that seems un-American for its patience, Phelps and his coach, Bob Bowman, have chucked instant gratification to work toward an audacious prospect for Beijing: Win it all.

"The only thing Michael can focus on now to improve his legacy or his swimming performance is 2008," Bowman says. "There's not much he can do in 2005 except get ready for 2008, and that's how I kind of look at it."

Coming back to earth

Gilding much of the pomp over Phelps last year was the promise his youth holds. The Mark Spitz standard, seven golds in one Games, still looms. Phelps has one, maybe two, more chances to clear it. He will be just 23 in Beijing.

Out of the pool, his aging process accelerated to a sprint the last 12 months. From promotional appearances to the DUI arrest to his first semester at the University of Michigan, where he would like to get a degree in sports management, Phelps went from a somewhat carefree teen living with his mom in suburban Baltimore to a young adult juggling responsibilities.

"I've seen him have to grow up pretty quickly," says American Ian Crocker, Phelps' nemesis in the 100 fly who, because they have the same agent, has spent a lot of time doing appearances with Phelps. "He's got a lot of hats he wears. I've seen him do a pretty good job of balancing all that."

Crocker and Phelps went almost directly from Athens to a U.S. bus tour. Phelps also did the overnight celebrity circuit, including *The Tonight Show*. By the time he arrived in Indianapolis in early October for the world short course championships, his back was stiff, his focus frayed. Phelps won his first race, the 200 free, then withdrew.

The back injury was not serious but kept him out of the pool for five weeks. During

Phelps on his way to winning the 400-meter individual medley final in world record time at the 2008 U.S. Olympic Team Trials at the Qwest Center in Omaha, Nebraska.

that time, on Nov. 4, he ran a stop sign in Salisbury, Md., where he was visiting friends. A state trooper pulled him over and administered roadside sobriety tests and a Breathalyzer. Phelps recorded a blood-alcohol level of 0.08, the legal limit in Maryland for driving under the influence.

"I think it was kind of easy after Athens to feel like maybe he operated in a little different set of rules than the average person," says Bowman, who has coached Phelps for nine years. "I think that kind of brought him down to earth in a rather dramatic way, but certainly a demonstrative way."

Prosecutors agreed to drop the DUI charge when Phelps pleaded guilty to the lesser driving while impaired. He was fined $250 and sentenced to 18 months' probation, including speaking at several Maryland schools. Last weekend he did his third and final Wicomico County community-service appearance.

"What I wanted to do was afterwards just come and say it, man up to making a mistake

and learning from it and helping other people not to make that mistake," Phelps says. "A year ago, I don't know if I would have done that or not."

Getting used to new routines

By December, he had moved to Ann Arbor to join Bowman, the Wolverines' new men's swim coach. Phelps bought a townhouse and enrolled in two spring classes, public speaking and kinesiology.

The transition from childhood friends and coming home to an empty place, where he has to do his laundry and cooking, was rocky, he says. He found peace in the pool.

"It's always been sort of his refuge," Bowman says. "It's also a world where he does everything right, and everybody tells him that and tells him, 'You're the greatest.'"

Because he's a professional athlete, Phelps is not eligible to compete for the University of Michigan. But as a volunteer assistant coach, he does train with the

Wolverines, an arrangement that pushes him as much as it does them.

"I'm not used to training with somebody next to me and racing every single day, every single stroke," says Phelps, who adds that his turns, traditionally one of the weaker parts of his swims, "have been coming around" because of the challenge.

Phelps also is practicing relays with the Michigan swimmers. That, with his attention on the 100 free, could help quiet the questions that frothed when the 2004 Olympic coaches put him on the 400 free relay team even though he didn't swim the 100 free individually in Athens. The team finished third.

"Michael still has a long way to go with regards to developing his relay expertise," Salo says. "A lot of that is his lack of doing a lot of the relays, as much as the college guys do. ... Their relay- exchange speed is so much better than Michael's generally is. I think Michael sees that he needs to improve that aspect of his skill, and certainly having that experience is going to help the coaches a lot more."

Ultimately, it also could help Phelps in his pursuit of perfection at Beijing. If the USA wins all three relays — in Athens the U.S. men won handily in the 400 medley relay and narrowly in the 800 free relay — it puts the brass ring of eight golds well within the reach of his extraordinary wingspan.

But those are debates and medal tallies for three years hence. Phelps is likely to make fewer headlines with his current mantra: "Baby steps to Beijing."

"We've kind of put him in a situation where maybe people are going to see he really has goals other than to make sure he wins a gold medal every time," Bowman says.

Phelps is making sure he's ready to win gold at the time when the world again will be watching. ✎

Phelps on his way to winning the 200-meter butterfly final at the 2008 U.S. Olympic Team Trials.

Phelps harnesses motivation for '08 Games

Indefatigable star uses positives and negatives to fuel fire

By Vicki Michaelis • Date: June 20, 2006

Michael Phelps' coach calls him "the motivation machine."

"He's motivated by failure, he's motivated by success, he's motivated by money, he's motivated by comments people make," Bob Bowman says. "He can take just about anything he comes across and turn it into some kind of motivation. That's one of his greatest attributes."

Phelps hasn't had to look far for an impetus since last year's world championships. There, testing the waters in the 400- and 100-meter freestyle, the 2004 Olympic star slipped from superhuman status. He failed to qualify for the 400 final and finished seventh in the 100.

"I did new things. I didn't like how they worked. And I saw that my times aren't where they should be, in my opinion, so from there, if it doesn't show me that I need to start getting back to serious training and start getting back into it, then I don't know what would," Phelps says.

The serious training included 18,400 meters, or nearly 11½ miles, of swimming one day last month at the U.S. Olympic Training Center in Colorado Springs. It was Phelps' hardest training day ever, Bowman says.

It was part of the prelude to a full summer schedule for Phelps that continues this weekend with a Grand Prix event in Santa Clara, Calif., and likely ends in mid-August in the

Phelps celebrates after winning the 400-meter individual medley final in world record time on June 29, 2008 at the U.S. Olympic Team Trials.

Pan Pacific championships in Victoria, British Columbia.

Phelps won five individual events, the 100 free among them, at a Charlotte meet two weeks ago and helped set two meet records in relays for Club Wolverine (Mich.). He finished second in one of his weakest events, the 200 breaststroke.

"I think this summer he feels a strong need to show that if he's not better than he was before, at least he's as good," Bowman says.

One of the main story lines in the 2008 Olympics figures to be whether Phelps is good enough to match or surpass the eight medals he won in 2004.

Olympic broadcaster NBC has asked the International Olympic Committee to switch the 2008 swimming finals from evenings to mornings so the races can be broadcast live in prime time. China is 12 hours ahead of Eastern Standard Time.

The IOC executive board is scheduled to discuss the request Thursday.

Bowman said a change could positively affect Phelps' Olympic performance. In 2004, Phelps had days in which he swam two preliminary races in the morning, then a semifinal and final at night.

"Obviously, the final is going to be most emotionally draining," Bowman says. "To have that first in the day I think is an advantage. ... Now he can feel free in the mornings

to just really go for it."

If the IOC approves the switch, Bowman plans to schedule morning finals the next two years at the Grand Prix event he helps organize as the University of Michigan coach. A change could have an effect on Phelps' Olympic program, though at next year's world championships, scheduled for March in Melbourne, Australia, Phelps' events likely will mirror those he swam in Athens.

That would mean leaving the 400 and 100 freestyle off the program — the 400 likely for good and the 100 until after the 2008 Games, Bowman says.

Phelps won gold in the 100 and 200 butterfly, the 200 and 400 individual medley, the 4x200 freestyle relay and the medley relay. He won bronze in the 200 freestyle and the 4x100 freestyle relay.

"You always say, 'Stick with what works,'" Phelps says, "but I never know what's going on in Bob's head. I'd like to try to do the same order. I don't know if the order is going to be different in Beijing."

Phelps' 2008 plans will be more definite after the 2007 worlds. For now he's consumed by a more short-term focus.

"I don't want to have another summer where I'm not happy afterward," he says. ✎

Showing little if any bluster, Phelps was quietly focused on breaking all-time records at the Beijing Olympics.

Phelps' Olympic dream, Phase 2

Swimmer seeks more glory in '08

By Vicki Michaelis • Date: February 13, 2007

Michael Phelps' newest companion, a 10-month-old English bulldog named Herman, isn't really a morning creature.

"When the alarm goes off in the morning for workout," Phelps says, "he'll look up at me and he's almost squinty-eyed, like, 'What are you doing up?'"

Phelps is rising early to build on his legacy.

He won six gold among eight Olympic medals in 2004, the most overall for anyone at a non-boycotted Games, as well as two individual world titles. He holds three individual world records.

His last preparatory meet for the March 25-April 1 world championships in Melbourne, Australia, comes this weekend at the Grand Prix of Swimming in Columbia, Mo. At worlds, fans will see a taller Phelps (he grew three-quarters of an inch in the year after the 2004 Olympics, to 6' 4") who is more muscular (up to 199 pounds) and more world-wise.

The 21-year-old believes the next 18 months, beginning in Melbourne and ending with the 2008 Summer Olympics in Beijing, "could really make me or break me as an athlete."

At first blush, that seems the kind of overstatement an overachiever uses as incentive to ease off the snooze button. Yet Phelps' performances over the next 18 months could make or break the arguments for whether he becomes the greatest swimmer.

Phelps does the breaststroke during a preliminary heat in the 400-meter individual medley at the 2008 U.S. Olympic Team Trials.

With the recent retirement of Australian great Ian Thorpe, the path to that title is clearer, although fellow U.S. Olympian Klete Keller contends Phelps "already passed" Thorpe.

"To really have a legacy that (Phelps) may be individually proud of, he's going to have to do it over more than one Olympics," three-time Olympic gold medalist and NBC swimming commentator Rowdy Gaines says.

Like Phelps, three modern-era male swimmers have had one dominant Olympics apiece: Thorpe, with three golds and two silvers on home soil at the 2000 Summer Olympics in Sydney; Matt Biondi, with five golds and seven overall medals in 1988; and Mark Spitz, with seven golds at the 1972 Games.

Phelps plans to compete through the 2012 Summer Games in London, after which, he says, he will be done.

"He's got two more Olympics where he's going to bring massive amounts of medals in," says Erik Vendt, who finished second to Phelps in the 400-meter individual medley in Athens and trains with Phelps in Ann Arbor, Mich. "So if people don't think that he's the greatest swimmer of all time now, just by looking at the pure statistics of it, I think by the end of his career it will be a no-brainer."

Gaines believes Phelps will earn top-rung status long before then.

"If Michael just makes the Olympic team (for Beijing), to me he's the greatest swimmer in history," Gaines says. "That's all he has to do."

Heavier Olympic load?

That's likely not all he will do.

Phelps swam in five individual events and three relays in the last Olympics. In Beijing, says his coach, Bob Bowman, "He

could do more. I don't know if he will do more, but he could."

Possible additions include the 200-meter backstroke, in which Phelps ranked fifth in the world last year, and/or the 100-meter freestyle, where he was seventh. Either could add three more races to his Olympic program because of preliminary heats.

At the 2004 Olympics, Phelps competed individually in the 100- and 200-meter butterfly, the 200- and 400-meter individual medley and the 200-meter freestyle. He will duplicate that program at the upcoming worlds, "probably one of the biggest meets of my life. And 2008 is probably second. I need to have a good worlds in order to have a good Olympics."

Phelps lived with his mom near Baltimore when he rose to stardom in Athens. For more than two years he has been on his own in Ann Arbor. He moved there to continue training with Bowman, his longtime coach, who became the University of Michigan's head men's swimming coach in 2005.

Phelps encountered bumps on the road to independence. A DUI charge in November 2004 was later dropped when Phelps pleaded guilty to the lesser charge of driving while impaired and was sentenced to 18 months' probation. That included speaking at schools and attending a Mothers Against Drunk Driving panel.

At the 2005 worlds he failed to qualify for the 400-meter freestyle final and finished seventh in the 100-meter freestyle.

"That year was more of me playing around too much and me not taking things as seriously as I should have," Phelps says. "That was like a wake-up call. I'm glad it was there rather than (last summer's Pan Pacific championships, where he won five gold medals and set two individual world records) or this coming worlds or at the Olympics."

Phelps, as pictured here in November 2007, trains relentlessly at the University of Michigan's Canham Natatorium.

Life in Ann Arbor

Phelps enrolled as a student at Michigan — he can't swim for the school because he's a pro — and has taken classes toward a degree in sports management. Last fall, as his training, media and endorsement commitments ramped up, he dropped his courses and for now is a full-time swimmer.

He lives on Ann Arbor's main street, close to sandwich shops and restaurants, where he can feed his famously voracious appetite. He plays poker and video games and watches his beloved Baltimore Ravens. He dates a recent Michigan graduate, whom he declines to identify, in a relationship he describes as "on and off."

He trains with University of Michigan swimmers and others such as Keller and Vendt who are fellow members of Club Wolverine, giving him an elite level of competition daily.

"It's exciting because I can race someone every day," he says. "When one of the freshmen talks trash to you during a workout, that fires you up."

He also is a full-time owner of Herman, a birthday gift last year from Phelps' agent. Between training times and competitions, Phelps is juggling dog care. He took a red-eye flight back from a swim meet in California last month to pick up Herman from his sister's house outside Washington, D.C.

"I guess it's pretty much what I thought it was going to be like," he says. "I always want to play with him, and when he wants to play, he plays. If I'm sitting on the couch watching TV, he's sitting there next to me, watching TV with me."

In August 2008, Herman can watch Phelps swim toward more history in Beijing. Phelps figures the 2008 Olympics will be the last in which he can swim his trademark ambitious program and therefore his last chance "to bring new attention to the sport."

"After '08, as of right now, I don't see myself swimming anything over 200 [meters]," Phelps says.

He doesn't think about his place in swimming history, he says. He wants to leave his name in swimming's record books, but he would rather his mark on sports be more widely felt.

"I remember Michael Jordan's hand on the Gatorade bottle, and it was huge. And I always would go to the grocery store, and I would measure up my hand against it," Phelps says. "It's something I always did when I was walking around the grocery store with my mom.

"It's little things like that that got kids excited about sports. That's what made him one of the best basketball players and athletes of all time, in my opinion."

What makes the greatest swimmer of all time? It starts with that doggone alarm. ✎

Phelps swims in the men's 100-meter butterfly preliminary at the 2008 U.S. Olympic Team Trials in Omaha, Nebraska.

Phelps might be 'greatest swimmer'

American breaks world records by wide margins

By Vicki Michaelis • Date: April 2, 2007

MELBOURNE, Australia — On video monitors at the world swimming championships, a superimposed world-record line — like the one used as a first-down marker in football — moved with the swimmers across the pool as they raced their final laps.

Most swimmers chased the line. They would appear to grasp at it, stroke after stroke, until it beat them to the wall.

One swimmer constantly overtook the line. Once by a full body length.

"It was behind his feet," U.S. coach Eddie Reese said of Michael Phelps' finish in the 200-meter butterfly, shaking his head in disbelief.

That line was Phelps' only competition in three finals in this worlds, which he finished Sunday with an unprecedented seven gold medals and five world records. His performance was so superlative it did the seemingly impossible: It pushed expectations for a swimmer who won six golds and eight overall medals in the 2004 Olympics, a record at a non-boycotted Games, even higher for the 2008 Beijing Games.

Even though Mark Spitz broke a world record in every event he entered in the 1972 Olympics (100 and 200 freestyle, 100 and 200 butterfly and three relays), U.S. head coach Mark Schubert said Phelps' performance is non-pareil because of his versatility in swimming the individual medleys as well as the

In swims leading up to Beijing, Phelps appeared to be unbeatable.

200 freestyle and 100 and 200 butterfly.

"His performance this week was the greatest performance of all time," Schubert said. "I just didn't notice any weak points. He can do it from behind, he can do it from in front, he can do it when it's close, he can do it when it's not close."

Nearly perfect meet

It also left those in his wake awed and reverential.

"He's unbelievable — by far the greatest swimmer of all time," said Albert Subirats Altes, who finished behind Phelps and the USA's Ian Crocker in the 100 butterfly to win the first world swimming medal for Venezuela.

The Netherlands' Pieter van den Hoogenband, who won the 2000 Olympic gold and 2004 silver in the 200 freestyle, is thinking about dropping the event from his 2008 program after finishing more than two seconds behind Phelps' world-record of 1 minute, 43.86 seconds here.

"I was next to him, I know how fast it is, and you have to be realistic," van den Hoogenband said. "I don't think in 18 months I will make that big a step."

The only question Phelps, 21, left dangling after eight days of jaw-dropping swims is how big a step he still can make before Beijing.

"The sky is the limit," van den Hoogenband said.

Phelps, after surprising himself night after night, had to agree.

"I'm excited to try to imagine a little bit more than I have in the past," he said when he finally was able to exhale Sunday, "and hopefully some more things are possible next year."

Phelps was on track to win eight golds until Crocker's false start Sunday in the 4x100 medley relay preliminaries disqualified the USA. Eight golds would have topped Spitz's seven in the 1972 Olympics. As it was, seven gave Phelps a record world championship total. Ian Thorpe held the record with six golds in the 2001 worlds.

"Everything can't go perfect," Phelps said about the relay error.

Except for Crocker leaving just one-hundredth of a second early on the relay exchange, though, everything did go nearly perfect for Phelps. He obliterated van den Hoogenband and Thorpe's world record in the 200 freestyle and touched out Crocker in the 100 butterfly.

He broke world records not by slim margins but by yawning gaps. In his last race, the 400 IM, he broke his world record by more than two seconds and beat silver medalist Ryan Lochte by more than three seconds.

Working toward Beijing

Phelps was so dominant it's hard to imagine what will drive him through the early wake-up calls and 80,000-meter training weeks before Beijing.

"How tired I am right now," he said in

response to the question Sunday. "Honestly, fatigue started really setting in three days ago. I think at the Olympics, it's going to be even harder, because the amount of pressure, the amount of press and everything that goes into the Olympics itself, I think, is more emotionally draining than a world championships is. There's work to be done to get ready for that."

That work involves consistent, hard training, as well as putting Phelps in stressful situations. At two warm-up meets for worlds, for example, Phelps swam the 100 backstroke, 100 breaststroke and 100 freestyle — none of which are his specialty — within an hour of one another.

"At this point," said Phelps' coach, Bob Bowman, "he knows what the pressure is, he knows what the expectations are, he's already done it once before, so I don't think that's something that I worry about with

him too much. My main concern with Michael is that he's impeccably prepared."

Bowman's concerns also lie in the details. While the rest of the world saw Phelps beat Lochte by more than a second and set a world record in the 200 IM final, Bowman saw room for improvement.

Coming off the last turn, Bowman said after studying the race, Phelps stayed underwater for 8.25 meters.

"It probably should have been 10 or 11," Bowman said.

Those are the kinds of details Bowman and Phelps will be working on for the next 16 months, as the world muses over what could be in Beijing. That's not to say Phelps won't consider the big picture, as he listens to one of his rap favorites, Notorious B.I.G's "Sky's The Limit".

"Every time I hear that, I really do think that," he said. "Anything is possible." ❧

Olympic workers walk through the midday heat in front of a giant mural of Phelps in the Olympic Green area of the Beijing Olympic Games.

New suit makes a splash

The best swimmer in the world is about to get better

By Janice Lloyd • Date: February 12, 2008

When Michael Phelps flies off the block in the new Speedo LZR Racer this weekend at the Missouri Grand Prix meet, he will be racing in a bodysuit he's spent the last two years helping develop with his coach Bob Bowman.

"It's true I've never worn a faster suit than we're about to wear," Phelps said. "It's definitely going to change a lot of records in the record books."

The suit will be unveiled today at a news conference in New York City and is expected to be worn by most U.S. swimmers and swimmers from more than 50 countries at the Beijing Olympics in August. Phelps gets a $1 million bonus from Speedo if he wins seven golds, a record held by American Mark Spitz. Phelps left Athens in 2004 with six golds and eight medals overall wearing a Speedo.

He won seven golds en route to setting five world records while wearing yet a different Speedo at worlds last April. Bowman said this suit's difference is "substantial" in terms of the surface and fitting.

"To know you're going to be in the best technology out there gives the athletes that little edge," Bowman said. "And that's what you need sometimes in the Olympic Games. The margins of victory are small."

Speedo claims this product has 10 percent "less passive

Phelps poses in the new Speedo LZR racer swimsuit following a news conference introducing the high-technology suit, in New York in February 2008.

drag" than the Fastskin launched before the 2004 Olympics. The ultra-lightweight fabric is water repellent. Welding allows a seamless fit. The LZR is the first suit Speedo developed with NASA.

"It's like a spacesuit," Phelps said. "When people are traveling through space, they're going ridiculously fast. That's what it feels like to me."

He has been testing prototypes at Michigan's pool in Ann Arbor, where he trains with Bowman and where Speedo's senior vice president of marketing, Stu Isaac, lives.

"I remember the first time Michael dove into our diving well at Michigan with the bodysuit on. It seemed that he went across the pool like a torpedo," Bowman said.

Isaac, a former Michigan coach, said test-ing with 20 other elite athletes has advanced to determine the suit's physiological impact: "We tested to make sure it didn't have any negative effects, such as raising body temperature or constricting the chest."

Constriction is so not an issue, said Jason Rance, head of Speedo's Aqualab, that "athletes are wearing tighter and tighter suits because they want the skintight fit and the hydrodynamic form."

Phelps laughed and wouldn't make any predictions about wearing the suit this weekend, although he set a world record there last year.

"We're all pretty excited to be able to wear the LZR in Missouri," Phelps said, "and hopefully we'll be able to do some fast times." ✎

(opposite) From head to toe, the new suit seemed to make the fastest swimmer in the world even faster. (above) Of course, it's what's inside the suit that matters, and Phelps works hard in the weight room to maintain his physique.

Phelps' recipe:

Mix most talent with best work ethic; just add water

By Christine Brennan • Date: July 1, 2008

OMAHA — It was Michael Phelps' 23rd birthday on Monday, so he is to be forgiven for rewarding himself with what amounted to a day off at the U.S. Olympic swimming trials. A 200-meter freestyle preliminary swim in the morning; another 200-meter freestyle semifinal swim at night. That's it.

For many of the 1,200 swimmers at the trials, two races would constitute their entire meet.

For Phelps, they are 10 percent of his workload here. Which is why a day with just two swims, rather than four (Friday) or five (Thursday), if all goes as planned, is a day that looks more like a vacation than a competition for the world's most impressive swimmer.

Because Phelps is not a complex man, because what you see from the 6' 4" "little" brother with the two older sisters and the adoring single mom is pretty much what you get, most of his story will be told in numbers. It will be numbers of medals to be won, numbers of world records to be set, or just plain old numbers, like 4:05.25, the world record he set in his first event Sunday, the men's 400 individual medley.

Phelps' life is swimming, and swimming is governed by these statistics. The numbers — world records almost across the board for a man who could win up to nine medals at the upcoming Beijing Olympics — do tell a story, though. It's a tale of dedication that is almost unprecedented in the annals of a

Phelps worked relentlessly leading up to Beijing to ensure that his performances would live up to the hype.

sport known best for demanding nothing but undying devotion from its athletes. Elite swimmers get up before dawn almost every day from childhood through college to then put their head in the water for hours on end, lap after laborious lap. Enough said?

But there's more.

Often, those with the most talent in a sport are not its hardest workers. But in at least two major American sports, we have in the past decade seen the ascent of the most talented athlete, perhaps ever, who also is willing to work the hardest. Golf has given us Tiger Woods. Swimming has given us Phelps. And we can see the results: stifling domination that often defies description.

Neil Walker, a 32-year-old Olympic gold medalist who has been on various relay teams with Phelps, tried to find an explanation Monday.

"He trains harder than anyone in the world," Walker said. "Bob Bowman (Phelps' coach) tells lots of stories. He does not take a day off, ever: Sundays, on a day when he's sick, never. He doesn't miss a day. That can be years of extra training over time. And, of course, he's perfecting his stroke when he's training."

Superlatives can sound superficial, but the truth is Phelps is a truly extraordinary competitor. After Phelps won six gold medals and two bronze medals at the 2004 Athens Olympics, one of the finest performances in Olympic history in any sport, he and Bowman decided he needed to work harder to get better. Others might balk. Not Phelps.

At the 2007 world championships, he won seven gold medals, breaking five world records in the process, and likely would have won an eighth gold had the U.S. men not been disqualified in the medley relay because of a false start.

A cynic would remind us that this is the steroid era in sports, so what can we believe anymore? It's a timely pre-Olympic question, for sure. But if there's any athlete on earth whose performances you can trust, it's someone like Phelps, who underwent 59 U.S. Anti-Doping Agency tests from 2001 through the end of June 2007 (the most recent statistical period), including many of the unannounced, knock-on-the-door variety. He has been tested internationally countless more times.

Here this week, competitive pitfalls abound, even for Phelps. Nothing is guaranteed. But Phelps is the kind of guy who lets his coach handle all the strategy, who laughs more than he frowns, who doesn't sweat the small stuff.

"Swimming all these events, he is helped by having a great ability to compartmentalize," said John Naber, who won four swimming gold medals at the 1976 Olympics. "That's what it takes to do well in multiple events. He goes one step at a time, then puts it in a box, then moves on." ꕥ

Phelps digs deep for one more squat during high-altitude conditioning camp at the U.S. Olympic Training Center in Colorado Springs, Colo.

Built to swim, Phelps found a refuge in water

Kid who "never sat still" aims for eight more golds

By Vicki Michaelis • Date: August 1, 2008

Michael Phelps' remarkably long torso is like the hull of a boat, his coach says, allowing him to ride high on the water. His ankles, knees, elbows and shoulder joints are rubber-band flexible. His wingspan is 3 inches longer than his 6' 4" height.

But for all of the genetic gifts that make him a master at defying drag in the water, for all of the physical advantages that could propel the 23-year-old swimmer in the next month to the best Olympic performance of all time, the key to Phelps' superiority is what is in his mind as he races.

Very little.

"It's either nothing or 'I have to get my hand on the wall before they do,'" says Phelps, who won six gold and two bronze medals in the 2004 Olympics.

His coach says that single-mindedness, that ability to shut out the great expectations and the supercharged Olympic atmosphere, will allow Phelps — who will race up to 20 times in Beijing in pursuit of a record eight gold medals — to climb out of the pool each time with an eye only on what's next.

"That," coach Bob Bowman says, "is his strongest attribute."

For an athlete who took Ritalin for attention deficit hyperactivity disorder (ADHD) as a child, it is also his most surprising asset.

Phelps' legendary size-14 feet look like flippers as he walks onto the platform before a swim at the 2008 U.S. Olympic Team Trials on July 3, 2008.

"Michael's ability to focus amazes me," says his mom, Debbie Phelps, a middle school principal who occasionally speaks on panels about ADHD. It's a condition that most frequently affects children, making it hard for them to pay attention to one thing or to sit for long periods.

Bowman, who began coaching Phelps at the North Baltimore Aquatic Club when the swimmer was 11, recalls how much time Phelps spent sitting near the lifeguard stand as a kid, benched because he was being too disruptive.

"He never sat still. He never shut up. He would never stop asking questions," his mom says. "He just wanted to go from one thing to another."

When he was in elementary school, a teacher told his mom that Phelps would never focus on anything. His mom disagreed. She had seen him at swim meets.

"He might be rocking on the kickboard as he's waiting to swim," she told the teacher, "but he knows what he wants to do."

Even then, Phelps pined to excel in the sport his mom initially chose for his energetic older sisters, Whitney and Hilary, now 28 and 30.

"I don't want to lose," Phelps says. "That's the thing. If I don't want to lose, I can focus."

Working toward a goal

Swimming wasn't just the family's pastime, it was its refuge. When Phelps was 9, his parents divorced, and his mom was grateful for the structure swimming provided. Hilary would become a college swimmer. Whitney nearly made the 1996 Olympic team before chronic back problems ended her career.

Under Bowman's guidance, their little brother grew from poolside pest into the world's best swimmer. The two have been together for 12 years, sometimes butting heads but more often blending Bowman's demanding, analytical approach with Phelps' talent and drive.

Both reject the notion that Bowman was a father figure while Phelps grew up with a single mom. In fact, they now refer to themselves as "business partners."

But Phelps acknowledges that Bowman helped him mature in and out of the pool.

"He, I guess, saw something in me ... and really has never given up on me, through good times and bad," Phelps says. "He's been able to help me grow from the little 11-year-old swimmer who didn't really know what he was doing to the person I am today."

Before Bowman entered the picture, Phelps already was turning heads — and flashing his aversion to losing.

Early on, his competitive streak wasn't pretty. He threw his goggles on the pool deck after his first loss, sparking a prolonged conversation with his mother about what he could have done instead.

Phelps made the Olympic team as a

15-year-old entrant in the 200-meter butterfly in 2000. When he finished fifth in Sydney, he was angry he hadn't won a medal. But instead of throwing his goggles, he immediately began training again.

"Not accomplishing a goal, no matter what it is for me, just makes me want it that much more," Phelps says.

"When I didn't medal, I was like, 'All right, well, then I'm going to do this.'" Within seven months, he set a world record in the 200 butterfly.

Even now, Phelps trains every day — including Sundays, figuring it gives him 52 more days a year in the pool than many of his competitors.

In peak training phases, Phelps will swim at least 80,000 meters a week, nearly 50 miles. That includes two practices a day, sometimes three when he's training at altitude.

"His motivation is that he just hates to lose," says U.S. teammate Ian Crocker, who will race against Phelps in Beijing in the 100 butterfly. "He's got a lot of biological advantages plus that desire."

Phelps' physical advantages make him seem gangly and uncoordinated on dry land. With short legs that give him a 30-inch inseam — the same as Bowman, who is 5 inches shorter — he is not a fluid runner. His fingertips dangle nearly at his knees.

Phelps admits to feeling like a fish out of water when out of the pool, citing the right wrist he broke last October while catching himself in a fall.

"If I could sleep in the water and not leave it, that's probably my safest bet," he says. "I would never get hurt. I would never have any problems."

In the water, his short legs, with his double-jointed knees and pliable ankles attached to size 14 feet, help him undulate like a dolphin. His long arms, combined with the flexibility in his shoulders and elbows, extend the reach of his strokes, which are powerful and rhythmic.

"When I first saw Michael, in '96, I looked at his stroke, I looked at his body type and said, 'This kid is going to be awesome,'" says Jon Urbanchek, who worked with Bowman and Phelps the last four years after Bowman succeeded him as the men's swimming coach at the University of Michigan.

Indeed, in the 2004 Olympics, Phelps was awesome.

His eight medals were the most in one Games for any athlete in a non-boycotted Olympics. But the two bronze medals in that haul, from the 200 freestyle and 4x100 freestyle relay, left him short of Mark Spitz's seven golds in the 1972 Olympics.

"I would have liked it, but there's a time and place for everything, and that wasn't the time or the place, I guess," Phelps says.

The time could be now. Spitz, for one, thinks so.

"This is going to be history," Spitz says. "He's going to do, as we say, a little schooling to the rest of the world."

Improving at a record pace

Phelps will swim the same events he did in Athens — the 200 and 400 individual medleys, the 100 and 200 butterfly, the 200 freestyle and three relays — a program that yielded seven golds in last year's world championships in Melbourne, Australia. An eighth gold fell out of reach when the U.S. 4x100 medley relay was disqualified for a false start.

His body's ability to recover quickly allows Phelps to swim as many races as he does. During some sessions in Beijing, he will have two races with less than an hour in between.

Measurements of Phelps' lactate levels — the body produces lactate when muscle cells use oxygen — just after his races are similar to those most people have when they are resting.

Bowman says that means Phelps is using his aerobic power more than his muscles, which would take longer than his lungs to recover.

Phelps also has learned to give measured effort throughout meets, conserving energy in preliminary and semifinal races. Bowman marvels at his ability to relax the muscles he's not using.

"When I'm swimming, I can make myself relax in any way, whether it's 'don't kick' or 'don't pull as hard,'" Phelps says. "In the prelim of a race, I won't use as much legs. I'll just do what I have to do to get in the finals."

In the 2007 worlds, Phelps didn't just win his individual races, he dominated, smashing five world records. Much of his speed came off his turns.

"What you clearly saw in Melbourne is Michael was the best in the world from the time his feet hit the wall until he takes his first stroke," Bowman says.

Phelps began lifting weights in 2005, which has given him a more powerful push off the wall.

In races, Phelps now travels more than 10 meters from the wall, where "you're going faster than you could ever swim," Bowman says, before taking a stroke. Other swimmers average 6 or 7 meters on turns.

"How do you beat that?" asks Matt Biondi, the American swimmer who won a total of 11 medals, including eight gold, over three Olympic Games. "When your lungs are burning and you can hardly feel your arms and you're battling a guy head-to-head, and then all of a sudden he gets a turbo boost and you've got to run him down?"

In Melbourne, no one came close to running down Phelps. Even his mom couldn't believe it.

"I was in awe," she says. "It was like, 'Michael, what are you doing?'"

Through it all, Phelps says, his mind was focused on simply touching the wall first. Even in practice, he doesn't let his mind wander far. As he swims lap after lap, he

says, he might sing a song in his head.

But his thoughts don't drift, he says, to his interests outside the pool, which include poker, video games and his beloved English bulldog, Herman.

When he walks on the pool deck for a race, rap or hip-hop likely is pumping through his headphones. "(But) my mind is focused on the job that I have to do," he says.

"It's just easy for me to do that. I don't know why."

All his mom knows is that swimming set her hyperactive son on a singular path. He asked to be taken off Ritalin when he reached middle school, mainly because he didn't want to go to the school nurse's office each day. His mom agreed on the condition he wouldn't act up at school.

By then, Bowman had laid out a plan for Phelps, one that had a horizon as far as the 2012 Olympics, one focused lap at a time. Phelps never went back on Ritalin.

"Would you look back and say, would any sport have done that? Maybe so," Debbie Phelps says. "But swimming was Michael's comfort zone." ❧

Mark Spitz presents Michael Phelps with the first-place medal during the ceremony for the 200-meter individual medley at the 2008 U.S. Olympic Team Trials in Omaha, Nebraska. Phelps won with a world record time of 1:54.80.

Phelps a world-beater with first gold

World-record swim in 400 IM his best race ever, coach says

By Vicki Michaelis; Mike Dodd • Date: August 11, 2008

BEIJING — Michael Phelps is ready to take on history.

He erased any doubt in his first final at the Beijing Olympics, winning the 400-meter individual medley in world-record time. His longtime coach, Bob Bowman, said it was Phelps' best race ever. "When you consider the circumstances, everything around it, to swim like that under that sort of expectation and pressure is pretty amazing," Bowman said.

Phelps could deliver the greatest performance in an Olympics. He has seven more events, beginning with the 4x100-meter freestyle relay, where a fast French team awaits the U.S. men, who set a world record (3 minutes, 12.23 seconds) in preliminaries.

If Phelps wins gold in them all, his medal haul would surpass swimmer Mark Spitz's record seven golds at the 1972 Olympics.

Phelps' 400 IM swim Sunday — in which he surged past his competitors on the breaststroke leg, normally his weakest stroke — only fed the anticipation.

"That was one of the most amazing swims I've ever seen in my life," teammate Aaron Peirsol said. "He just blew people away. He's going to be on fire."

Phelps finished in 4:03.84, lowering his own world record by more than a second, to beat silver medalist Laszlo Cseh of

Phelps swam to victory and gold in the 400-meter individual medley at the National Aquatics Center in Beijing. He broke the world record with a 4:03:84.

Hungary. The USA's Ryan Lochte won bronze.

"I think it lets us know that physically and mentally, he's in peak shape, and hopefully we can carry that forward," Bowman said.

As automatic as victories now seem for Phelps, who won six gold and two bronze medals at the 2004 Olympics and seven golds at last year's world championships, Sunday's win choked him up on the medal stand. "I was pretty emotional after that race," Phelps said. "I'm pretty excited to have the first one under my belt." ❧

4:03.84

Phelps' world record time in the 400-meter individual medley.

(opposite) Phelps swims the backstroke leg of the 400-meter individual medley final at the National Aquatics Center in Beijing. (above) American fans cheer on their swimming heroes at The Water Cube in Beijing.